TELEVISIONARIES

THE RED ARMY FACTION STORY
1963-1993
By Tom Vague

Vague 26 1994

AK PRESS
EDINBURGH   SAN FRANCISCO

V A G U E

Originally published in Vague 20, 1988
Revised and updated by AK Press 1994
This edition published 2005 by AK Press
                AK Press
                PO Box 12766
                Edinburgh
                Scotland EH8 9YE
                (0131) 555-5165
                www.akuk.com
                ak@akedin.demon.co.uk

                AK Press
                674-A 23rd Street
                Oakland, CA 94612-1163
                USA
                (510) 208-1700
                www.akpress.org
                akpress@akpress.org

Designed by brian design
Printed and bound in the USA

British Library Cataloguing-in-Publication Data
A catalogue record for this title is available from the British Library

Library of Congress Cataloging-in-Publication Data
A catalogue record for this title is available from the Library of Congress

ISBN 1 873176 47 3

'Whether 'tis nobler in the mind to suffer the slings and arrows of outrageous fortune, or to take arms against a sea of troubles, and by opposing end them?'

'Well, it's better than bottling it up.'

'These tactics will be condemned to theoretical hibernation if they cannot, by other means, attract collectively the individuals whom isolation and hatred for the collective lie have already won over to the rational decision to kill or kill themselves. No murderers – And no humanists either! The first accepts death, the second imposes it. Let ten people meet who are resolved on the lightning of violence rather than the agony of survival: From this moment despair ends and tactics begin. Despair is the infantile disorder of the revolutionaries of everyday life.'

RAOUL VANEIGEM, *THE REVOLUTION OF EVERYDAY LIFE*

'I've seen the horrors, horrors that you've seen. But you have no right to call me a murderer. You have a right to kill me. You have a right to do that. But you have no right to judge me... It's impossible for words to describe what is necessary to those who do not know what horror means. Horror. Horror has a face and you must make a friend of horror. Horror and moral terror are your friends. If they are not then they are enemies to be feared. They are truly enemies.

'I remember when I was with Special Forces, seems a thousand centuries ago, we went into a camp to innoculate children. We left the camp after we'd innoculated the children for polio and this old man came running after us and he was crying, he couldn't see. We went back there and they had come and hacked off every innoculated arm. There they were in a pile, a pile of little arms. And I remember I, I, I cried, I wept like some old grandmother, I wanted to tear my teeth out, I didn't know what I wanted to do, and I want to remember it, I never want to forget it. I never want to forget it. I never want to forget. And then I realised like I was SHOT, like I was shot with a diamond, a diamond bullet right through my forehead. And I thought my god, the genius of that, the genius, the will to do that. Perfect, genuine, complete, crystal, pure. Then I realised that they were stronger than we. Because they could – understand that they were not monsters, these were men, trained cadre, these men who fought with their hearts, who have families, who have children, who are filled with love. But they had THE STRENGTH – THE STRENGTH to do that.

'If I had ten divisions of those men then our troubles here would be over very quickly. You have to have men who are moral and at the same time who are able to utilise their primordial instincts to kill without feeling, without JUDGEMENT – without judgement – because it's judgement that defeats us.'

COLONEL WALTER E. KURTZ, *APOCALYPSE NOW!*

FROM THIS MOMENT DESPAIR ENDS AND TACTICS BEGIN

JUNE 2, 1967: THE SUMMER OF HATE - BURN WAREHOUSE BURN! - THE SHAH'S VISIT AND THE KILLING OF BENNO OHNESORG

In 1963 the USAF begin surface-bombing rural districts of South Vietnam. By 1965 B52s are bombing North Vietnamese cities...

FEBRUARY 5, 1965: 2,000 students march through West Berlin. 500 leave the main march and attack the US embassy. Afterwards posters go up asking: 'FOR HOW MUCH LONGER WILL WE TOLERATE MASS MURDER COMMITTED IN OUR NAME?'

EARLY 1967: Leading lights of the West Berlin student movement, Fritz Teufel, Dieter Kunzelmann (a former Situationist), Bommi Baumann and Rainer Langhans, form 'KOMMUNE 1'. Rudi Dutschke, the leader of the SDS (the Socialist Student Union) is also an early member but doesn't last long. Fritz Teufel is already famous in his own right for various student pranks, but K1 first hit the headlines when Hubert Humphrey visits Berlin in April.

The group plan to welcome the US Vice-President with custard pies, but the press gets hold of it and cries wolf with stories of bomb threats. In 'Konkret', Germany's answer to 'Oz', top columnist Ulrike Meinhof (Germany's answer to Julie Burchill) writes: 'It is thought rude to throw custard pies at politicians, but not to welcome politicians who have villages wiped out and cities bombed... napalm yes, custard no.'

K1 get a bit more serious in May. After a Brussels department store fire in which 300 die, a handout of theirs reads: 'When will the department stores of Berlin burn? The Yanks have been dying for Berlin in Vietnam. We were sorry to see the poor souls obliged to shed their

Rudi can't fail: Rudi Dutschke, leader of the SDS

coca-cola blood in the Vietnamese jungle. So we started by marching, throwing the occasional egg at America House and we would have liked to finish seeing HHH die smothered in custard. Now our Belgian friends have at last found the knack of really involving the whole population in all the fun of Vietnam... Brussels has given us the only answer: BURN WAREHOUSE BURN!'

SUMMER 1967: A great deal of publicity heralds the state visit to Berlin of the Shah of Iran and the Empress Farah Diba. Dieter Kunzelmann's contribution is: 'I do not study, I do not work, I have trouble with my orgasm, and I wish the public to be informed of this.' Ulrike Meinhof's is 'An Open Letter to Farah Diba' (in response to an interview the Empress gave to 'Neue Revue'): 'You say "Summers are very hot in Iran, and like most Persians I and my family travel to the Persian Riviera on the Caspian Sea." Like most Persians? Isn't that somewhat exaggerated? Most Persians are peasants with an annual income of less than $100. And for most Persian women every second child dies of starvation, poverty and disease. And the children too, those who knot carpets in their 14 hour day, do they too, most of them, travel to the Caspian Sea in summer?'

JUNE 2: After all the anti-Shah Iranians have been rounded up, the pro-Shah faction are allowed to greet their Emperor as he arrives in Berlin. When the Imperial cortege reaches Schöneberg City Hall, hundreds of student demonstrators have to be held back. The German police are assisted in this task by Iranian secret servicemen armed with long wooden staves.

That evening the Shah and Farah Diba arrive at the Opera House to some chanting and a few off-target bags of paint. The demonstrators drift off towards nearby bars, planning to return to see the Shah off. Suddenly 14 ambulances pull up blocking their escape route. The police dish out some heavy-handed crowd-control, far worse than the scenes in Schöneberg, and the ambulances are soon full. Then the mopping-up operation begins.

A handful of demonstrators make a last stand in Krummestr. with uniformed police lined up in front of them. A plain-clothes snatch-squad goes in to apprehend a 'ringleader'. They get their man and fling him to the ground. Thereupon other demonstrators surround the snatch-squad and uniformed police come to their aid. Hand-to-hand fighting breaks out and the suspected ringleader momentarily gets away. Then Det. Sgt. Karl-Heinz Kurras (of the 'Popo' – Political Police) points his 7.65mm pistol at the recaptured demonstrator's head. A shot rings out and Benno Ohnesorg, a 26 year-old romantic languages student, is dead.

June 2, 1967 is the turning point for a lot of people in Germany. Even Mayor Albertz is deeply affected (he quits office soon after of his own accord), but not the Shah, who tells Albertz, "not to think too much of it, these things happen every day in Iran." The quote of the night, however, comes from one of the demonstrators who'd escaped to the SDS centre: Gudrun Ensslin sums up what many of the battered students are feeling when she says "They'll kill us all. You know what kind of pigs we're up against. This is the Auschwitz generation. You can't argue with the people who made Auschwitz. They have weapons and we haven't. We must arm ourselves!"

The Shah adds further insult to injury by demanding that judicial action be taken against the demonstrators. In response hundreds of people turn up at police stations to plead guilty to demonstrating – But only Fritz Teufel is held; for plotting against Hubert Humphrey, throwing a stone at the Shah and inciting arson with 'Burn Warehouse Burn'. After a complaint is lodged with the state court, he too is released. However Teufel refuses to hand over his passport and demands to be let back into prison. Without a court order no-one will oblige. Finally he stages a 'go-in' on the Berlin State Parliament, which effectively gets him reincarcerated.

Andreas Baader isn't in Berlin for the Shah's visit. He's otherwise engaged at Traunstein borstal for stealing a motorbike. But he surfaces later that summer, meets Gudrun Ensslin for the first time and makes quite an impression on the 'Extra-Parliamentary Opposition'. He's described at the time as being more of a 'Marlon Brando type' than a student drop-out, who talks about little else but terrorism and stealing cars.

YOU CAN'T GO HOME AGAIN

1968: FIRE WALK WITH ME - THE FRANKFURT FIREBOMBINGS - THE SHOOTING OF
RUDI DUTSCHKE - THE SPRINGER SIEGE - THE ARSON TRIAL AND THE BATTLE OF
TEGELER WEG

MARCH 22, 1968: Teufel and Langhans are cleared of incitement to arson. The Kommune 1 handout is judged to be satire. Though not by Gudrun Ensslin and Andreas Baader, who visit K1 to see if anyone is into putting their ideas into practice. But no-one is except Thorwald Proll, a friend of Baader and Ensslin. The three of them drive to Munich, where they pick up Horst Söhnlein, an old Fassbinder-baiting pal of Baader's. (RWF: "I don't throw bombs: I make films.")

APRIL 2: After stopping off at Gudrun's volks in Stuttgart (incidentally Gudrun Ensslin is a descendant of Hegel), the group arrive in Frankfurt. Baader and Ensslin go into the Kaufhaus Schneider store, take the escalator up to the 3rd floor, try out a few camp beds, wander briefly round the other floors and leave. Then just before closing time they return. The store is almost empty and the couple are anything but discreet. They run up the switched-off escalators holding hands and, when they think no-one's looking, plant an incendiary device in the women's clothing department. A second bomb is placed in a cupboard in the furniture department and just before the store closes the couple run out into the street. More devices are planted that evening in the nearby Kaufhof store, but whoever is responsible makes a better job of concealing the fact.

Shortly before midnight the third and then the first floor of the Kaufhaus Schneider go up in flames. A few minutes later and the Kaufhof is also burning. Fire engines soon arrive at both stores, nobody is hurt and the damage is minimal ($250,000). Baader, Ensslin, Proll and Söhnlein hear the sirens from the 'Club Voltaire', a revolutionary

Frankfurt watering hole, and go out to join the crowd of onlookers. Afterwards a woman they know puts them up in her apartment.

The following evening they meet up again at Club Voltaire and take their host's child home, so she can stay on at the bar. The next morning, the Frankfurt police receive a tip-off and a few minutes later Baader, Ensslin, Proll and Söhnlein are arrested in the woman's apartment. The SDS disown the action but by and large K1 approve. As Bommi Baumann put it: 'It made no difference to me at the time whether they'd set fire to a store or not, what mattered was just that people had broken out of the system for once.'

APRIL 11: A week after the Frankfurt fire-bombings, an attempt is made on the life of Rudi Dutschke, the SDS leader. Josef Bachmann, a mentally sub-normal house painter, takes the inter-zone train from Munich to Berlin, apparently inspired by the neo-nazi 'Deutsche Nationale Zeitung' (a cutting from which is later found on his person, proclaiming 'Stop Dutschke Now!'). He finds Dutschke's address at the residents' registration office then lays in wait for him outside his apartment on the Ku-damm.

When Dutschke appears on his bike, Bachmann approaches him, asks if he is Rudi Dutschke, then calls him a "filthy communist swine" and shoots him three times. Dutschke falls off his bike, losing his shoes, but manages to get up and stagger towards the SDS centre, crying out "I have to go to the barber, I have to go to the barber." (According to 'Baader-Meinhof Group' author Stefan Aust anyway and he was there. And in the light of subsequent youth culture developments, this may have been the most important thing Rudi ever said.)

After the shooting Bachmann takes an overdose of sleeping pills and his life, like that of his victim, is only just saved in hospital. (For the record he succeeded in his second suicide attempt.) The over-riding mood on the Ku-damm and throughout Berlin is one of brooding anger, until it's announced on the 6.30 news that Dutschke has survived. Only then does the crowd gathered at the SDS centre act. An emotional meeting is held at the Technical University and the blame laid to rest on the shoulders of the right-wing Springer press. From the university the students march on the Springer building in Kochstr. chanting 'Springer out of Berlin! Bild fired the gun too!'

Ulrike Meinhof, who's at the SDS centre, drives her 'Konkret' colleague Aust to the Springer compound. When they arrive at the compound gates a student comes up to them and says more cars are needed to stop the Springer trucks getting out. Ulrike isn't too keen on her car being part of a barricade, but Aust tells her to park it on the pavement, so it will still be part of the barricade but won't block the road. However, the police make sure the trucks get through and Ulrike Meinhof is one of those charged with using force. Aust then comes to

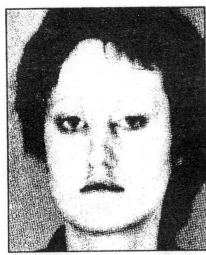

Ulrike Meinhof

Ulrike's assistance once again by managing to prove that her car wasn't causing an obstruction.

During the Springer siege molotovs used to set trucks alight are supplied by one Peter Urbach, who is later revealed to be an agent-provocateur in the employ of the government. In the same weekend a student and a press photographer are killed in vicious streetfighting in Munich; and Bommi Baumann is arrested for slashing tires and sentenced to nine months imprisonment. The Ulrike Meinhof column in the May 'Konkret' is entitled 'From Protest to Resistance'.

SUMMER 1968: The Dutschke assassination attempt is the spark for massive demonstrations in Berlin and Bonn, followed by strikes and occupations at almost every university in the BRD. The Frankfurt arsonists miss out on all this, awaiting trial in various remand centres. Andreas Baader writes to Kommune 1: 'And when Bonn has fallen, leave NATO for us...'

OCTOBER 14: The arson trial finally begins. Lawyers include Otto Schily, Horst Mahler and Gudrun's old professor Heinitz. When the judge first calls Baader, Thorwald Proll stands up instead. The judge proceeds to interrogate Proll until the state prosecutor tells him he has the wrong man. At which point both of them are ejected from court. Söhnlein fights his way out in solidarity and, when the judge sentences them to three days for bad behaviour, Proll shouts "I raise you to four!" On the third day of the trial Gudrun Ensslin makes a statement saying that she and Baader started the fires, in protest at indifference to the Vietnam war: 'We have found that words are useless without action.'

OCTOBER 31: All four defendants are sentenced to three years imprisonment. As their appeals go through, one of the lawyers, Horst Mahler is in court himself facing an application to stop his practice because of his part in the Springer demonstration. However the siege of the Springer compound pales in comparison to the scenes outside the Berlin court where his case is heard. In what becomes known as the 'Battle of Tegeler Weg', 130 police and 22 demonstrators are injured in the worst streetfighting ever seen in the BRD. For the first time rocker types join in on the side of the students, and the police receive their soundest beating to date. After Tegeler Weg police are issued

Proll, Söhnlein, Baader, Ensslin at their arson trial in 1968

with special riot shields, helmets and extra-long truncheons.

NOVEMBER 4: The Department of Internal Affairs in West Berlin is firebombed.

DECEMBER 19: The Rectorate of the University of West Berlin gets the same treatment.

INSTRUCTIONS FOR TAKING UP ARMS

1969/70: THE FRANKFURT APPRENTICES SCHEME - THE SCHILI AND THE RASPBERRY REICH - WAYS UNDERGROUND AND THE RECAPTURE OF BAADER

FEBRUARY 27, 1969: Richard Nixon's visit to West Berlin is greeted by more demos and an unsuccessful attempt to bomb his motorcade. Subsequent police raids uncover a bomb (supplied by Peter Urbach) and Dieter Kunzelmann and Rainer Langhans are arrested.

MARCH 9: JFK library in West Berlin firebombed.

APRIL: Ulrike Meinhof stops writing for 'Konkret'. The previous year she had divorced Klaus Rainer Röhl, the 'Konkret' publisher and left Hamburg for Berlin with their two daughters. Now the split is complete and it isn't very amicable. At one point Ulrike attempts to occupy the 'Konkret' office.

JUNE 13: Baader, Ensslin, Proll and Söhnlein are released on parole, under an amnesty for political prisoners. Baader and Ensslin end up at the 'Frankfurt Apprentices' Collective' – a popular student cause of the time is the plight of young people in state run homes (borstals). A large number of these 'apprentices' had run away and were living more or less underground, assisted by students; Baader gets on especially well with the apprentices because it isn't that long since he was one himself. And to the boys, Baader's practical experience is infinitely preferable to the political theories of the students. Baader organises 'sports activities', such as high-speed car chases round the inner-circle roads of Frankfurt and 'go-ins' on restaurants.

Baader says he wants to empty all the homes in the Federal Republic and unleash an army of thousands of inmates. Towards this end, he or Ulrike Meinhof take the original apprentices to visit other homes, recruiting and protesting about conditions. When finance isn't immediately forthcoming from the authorities, Baader and Ensslin find they can easily obtain donations from the chic-left or 'Schili' – lawyers, lecturers and the like (trendy lefties). Whenever funds get low, Gudrun's line is "Oh well, we've got to resort to writing begging letters to the liberal shits again." At weekends the two drive off to play on the consciences of the schili and return with gifts from the 'Raspberry Reich' – like a Mercedes from the wife of a Frankfurt boutique owner.

NOVEMBER: This quiet, relatively legal spell comes to an end, when the Federal High Court demands that Baader, Ensslin, Proll and Söhnlein return to jail. Only Horst Söhnlein obeys, the others decide to go underground. The three of them set off from Frankfurt in a friend's car. At Hanau they switch cars and drivers and go onto Saarbrücken, where the third and final getaway car is waiting to take them across the border into France.

The three spend the night at a schili house in Forbach, Lorraine and drive onto Paris in the morning. There a safe house in the Latin Quarter has already been found for them (belonging to Regis Debray, Che Guevara's comrade-in-arms, who's serving a 30 year sentence in Bolivia following Che's death in 1967). Once they're settled Baader rings Thorwald Proll's sister, Astrid and gets her to bring files, books and the Mercedes from Frankfurt. Thorwald meets her outside the Paris police HQ which is close to Debray's apartment.

For the next few days the four of them take it easy, hanging out in Parisian cafes, spending vast amounts of schili money and being recklessly driven about by Baader. Then Astrid Proll is sent off to Amsterdam to acquire false papers (and see 'Easy Rider') and on her return they hit the road again, heading south. In Strasbourg they dump Thorwald Proll, who eventually turns himself in like Horst Söhnlein. Neither of them have anything more to do with the group. Baader, Ensslin and Astrid Proll go onto Italy via Switzerland.

NOVEMBER/DECEMBER: Series of bomb attacks on American targets in West Berlin.

FEBRUARY 1970: A petition is made on Baader and Ensslin's behalf by the likes of Ulrike Meinhof and the director of the Frankfurt Youth Office; but it's rejected. When Gudrun Ensslin is told the news, over the phone in Naples, she says "Okay, we'll just have to carry on then." Then the lawyer Horst Mahler visits them in Italy and suggests they return to Berlin and form an underground group with him.

Astrid Proll eventually makes it back, after stealing an Alfa-Romeo in Rome (their own Mercedes had been stolen in Naples) and crashing in a snowstorm in Austria. Baader and Ensslin follow a few days later. Once again stopping off at Gudrun's volks in Stuttgart and even visiting the local carnival in disguise.

Meanwhile, Ulrike Meinhof is working on a film, 'Bambule'

Astrid Proll and Andreas Baader hang out in a Paris cafe

(Resistance) about the treatment of young people in custody. Apprentices from Frankfurt and their Berlin equivalent begin turning up at her door, and in due course the apprentices' hero, Andreas Baader and Gudrun Ensslin do too. 'Hans and Grete', as they're known to Meinhof's kids, stay at her Kufsteinerstr. apartment for two weeks.

During this time a loose association exists between Dieter Kunzelmann from K1/'Tupamaros West Berlin'/the 'Blues' (who is also wanted in connection with the November/December bombing campaign), the Horst Mahler group and Baader/Ensslin. But there is soon a clash over leadership between Baader and Kunzelmann. And an irreconcilable difference in style develops between the radical Maoist tactics favoured by Baader/Ensslin and the K1 prankster dope scene that 'the June 2nd Movement' is to come out of. So Baader makes his move on the Horst Mahler group, who have yet to make the all-important leap from theory into practice.

Horst Mahler's literal baptism of fire is the petrol bombing of administration offices in the Märkischer Viertel. Mahler's molotov actually misses but he's shown willing. Then he finds Baader and Ensslin new accommodation because Ulrike Meinhof's apartment is no longer considered safe. The entrance hall to the new apartment is furnished in a conventional manner, but the rooms only contain mattresses and bare essentials. Other apartments are rented and kept empty in reserve. The group is slowly expanding but Ulrike Meinhof remains a sympathetic observer, not yet ready to take the plunge because of her children.

Next on the agenda is arms. There's an aborted attempt to steal guns from the guards patrolling the wall, then Peter Urbach, the counter-intelligence man, is summoned. Urbach says he has a case of World War 2 guns buried in a Buckow cemetery. But when he takes Baader and Mahler to the cemetery they keep getting disturbed whenever they start to dig. The next day Baader is driving as recklessly as ever through Kreuzberg in Astrid Proll's Mercedes, when he gets stopped by the police. Although he's let off with a warning, the traffic cop later recognises him on a wanted poster. Soon 'Schupo' (Town Police), 'Bepo' (Young Reserves), 'Kripo' (Criminal) and 'Popo' (Political), the 'Anti-Marxist Brothers', are looking for Baader in Berlin.

APRIL 3: Urbach is given another chance to find his arms stash. This time they actually get to dig but strike paydirt. Urbach manages to talk his way out of it and they set off for home. Mahler and Urbach lead in the latter's car. As they're driving through Neukölln a Kripo radio car pulls up beside them. Mahler becomes very nervous but Urbach keeps driving. Then a second police car swings out in front of Astrid Proll's Mercedes and stops it.

Andreas Baader

Baader hands over an ID card and driving license in the name of 'Peter Chotjewitz'. The ID card has such details as how many children Herr Chotjewitz has. When the Kripo ask Baader this he gives the game away somewhat by saying he can't remember. He's then taken, along with Renate Wolff and Peter Homann – the other occupants of the Mercedes – for further ID checks. Baader is the only one detained, the others are allowed to leave.

Early the next morning, Horst Mahler calls the police and, in his capacity as Baader's lawyer, demands to know where he's being held. "If you can confirm that the person arrested earlier this morning actually is Herr Baader," comes the reply. Mahler has put his foot in it. For despite being a police station pin-up for some months, Baader hasn't been positively identified from his fingerprints. In any case it's extremely unlikely that Baader would have been released without further checks. As it is he's sent to Tegel prison to serve the remainder of his three years.

Urbach is now suspected of being a police infiltrator, though it seems the only repercussion is he isn't trusted anymore. Baader, however, isn't forgotten. He receives regular visits from Mahler, Mahler's secretary Monika Berberich, Ulrike Meinhof and 'Dr. Gretel Weitermeier' (Ensslin). And plans are soon afoot to spring him.

First Monika Berberich writes to the prison authorities, requesting permission for Baader to collaborate with Ulrike Meinhof on a book about 'young people on the fringe of society'. Then Ulrike Meinhof asks if Baader could be allowed to visit the 'German Institute for Social Issues' in Dahlem, to research the book. At first this request is denied but Horst Mahler, who also happens to be at Tegel, makes amends for his previous blunder by persuading the governor.

Meanwhile the problem of how to obtain arms is still unresolved. Finally the task is given to Hans-Jürgen Bäcker who, through his close ties to the Berlin criminal fraternity, comes up with the 'NPD', a neo-Nazi group. There's some deliberation on the ideological soundness of buying arms from Nazis, then Astrid Proll and Irene Goergens go to the 'Wolf's Lair' bar in Charlottenburg. There they meet a man called 'Teddy' (real name, Gunther Voigt), an arms dealer who had previously approached the proprietor. He takes them to a girlfriend's apartment where he keeps his stock, and sells them a Beretta and a Reck with silencers and ammunition for DM2,000.

THE JOB

OUTSIDERS - THE SPRINGING OF BAADER - ULRIKE MEINHOF MAKES THE LEAP - HOLIDAYS IN THE SUN - AND PLO BASIC TRAINING

MAY 14: Ulrike Meinhof arrives at the Dahlem Institute shortly after 8am, and settles down to work. At 9.30 Baader's prison car pulls up outside. His two guards check the windows of the reading room and agree to release Baader from his handcuffs so he can work. Then Irene Goergens and Ingrid Schubert are allowed in to look up some facts on juvenile delinquent therapy. They sit in the hallway pretending to work until the doorbell rings again. This time they get up to answer it and let in a man in a balaclava, brandishing a Beretta.

Librarian Georg Linke rushes into the hall and the masked man fires at him, putting a bullet in his liver. The librarian manages to get back into his office, then out of a window with his two secretaries. Meanwhile the masked man and a masked woman (Gudrun Ensslin) enter the adjoining office to the reading room and the man points his gun at librarian Frau Lorenz. The two girls, who now have their guns out, rush past him into the reading room.

As the startled guards get up, Baader opens a window and jumps out, closely followed by Ulrike Meinhof. The other four shoot tear gas and bullets into the room. The guards manage to get the gun from the man in the mask, but they can't stop him and the three girls following Meinhof and Baader out the window. Round the corner Astrid Proll is waiting for them in a stolen Alfa-Romeo.

The getaway car is later found by the Kripo with a tear-gas pistol and 'Introduction to Das Kapital' under the driving seat. Georg Linke is seriously wounded but he lives. Ulrike Meinhof's film 'Bambule', which was to be screened around this time, is struck from the schedule and never shown. Who killed Bambule? With her leap out of the window of the Institute, Ulrike ended her career as a successful journalist and started a new one as a notorious outlaw.

JUNE 2: 'Did the pigs really believe that we would let Comrade Baader languish in prison for two or three years? Did they really believe that we would talk about the development of class struggle and the re-organisation of the proletariat without arming ourselves at the same time? Did the pigs who shot first believe that we would allow ourselves to be shot like cattle without violence? Those who don't defend themselves die, those who don't die are buried alive in prisons, in reform schools, in the slums of worker districts, in the stone coffins of the new housing developments, in the crowded kindergartens and schools, in brand new kitchens and bedrooms filled with fancy furniture bought on credit. START THE ARMED RESISTANCE NOW! BUILD UP THE RED ARMY!'

JUNE 8: The Horst Mahler group (Hans-Jürgen Bäcker, Monika Berberich, Brigitte Asdonk, Manfred Grashof, Petra Schelm and Mahler) fly to Beirut from East Berlin. From Beirut they intend to go on to an Al Fatah training camp in Amman, Jordan; but their flight's delayed due to fierce fighting between the PLO and King Hussein. This means the Germans have to pass through the Lebanese checkpoint, and some of them only have Berlin ID cards. The official on duty decides to impound all their papers and holds the group in the customs office. After a while the official knocks off for the day and locks the Germans' papers in his desk.

Time for another blundering phone-call from Horst Mahler: this time to the French embassy, who he thinks are looking after East German interests. They are in fact only looking after West German interests. Mahler announces who and where he is before Petra Schelm realises who's at the other end and cuts him off. The French embassy duly inform the BRD, who order the Lebanese to arrest the group. However the Lebanese stall, not particularly wanting to upset the Palestinians, and a PLO troop arrive at the airport and release the Germans. Some fedayeen go to the house of the official, beat him up and demand the key to the desk. But someone else has it so they load the whole desk into a truck and take it with them.

Then the Mahler group are put in the Beirut Strand for the night. And that's where the Lebanese militia arrest them a few hours later, before returning them to the airport, where once again they are rescued by the Palestinians, who this time take them across the Syrian border to Damascus. There they receive some firearms training from the fedayeen before being driven on to Amman.

JUNE 21: A second group including Baader, Ensslin and Meinhof take the U-bahn to Friedrichstr. and cross over into East Berlin. There they disguise themselves as Arabs and proceed to Schönefeld airport. The PLO liaison man, Said Dudin brings United Arab Emirates passports

Gudrun Ensslin

this time, but they're still delayed and don't reach Damascus until the following afternoon. Then the Syrians refuse to let them in, but once again the Palestinians intervene and escort them over the Jordanian border.

At Amman the advance party greet them with hugs and kisses. Horst Mahler, sporting a Castro-style beard and cap, is very much the leader of the guerrilla band. But not for long: Baader immediately gives him a dressing down for making their trip frontpage news back in Germany. Mahler might have been a brilliant lawyer but he's no match for his venomous former client, and soon concedes leadership.

Then PLO basic training begins with a sort of revolutionary tourist programme (which many legal parties of European students undertook at the time). But the Baader/Mahler group insist on getting some real military training. Everyone is issued with combat gear (except Andreas Baader, who goes through basic training in skintight trousers) and armed with a Kalashnikov, because the camp is under constant threat of attack. (A few weeks after the embryonic RAF leave Amman, the camp and most of its occupants are wiped out in 'Black September'.)

Baader soon makes sure that the training is altered to suit 'The Job', as he calls their proposed urban guerrilla activities. This includes instruction in 'How to rob a bank', which the Algerian camp commandant, Achmed has first hand experience of in the Algerian war of independence. But it doesn't take long for Baader and Achmed to fall out. Baader demands to be treated on an equal footing to the Palestinian leader Abu Hassan. When Achmed ignores this demand, Baader calls a training strike.

During the strike some of the German girls sunbathe naked on the roof of their quarters. This causes some consternation among the young fedayeen, most of whom have never seen a woman naked before. Achmed puts his foot down, shouting "What do you think this is? This isn't a tourist beach!" To which Baader counters "The anti-imperialist struggle and sexual emancipation go hand in hand, fucking and shooting are the same thing!"

But for once Baader has met his match and the strike is called off. Then Abu Hassan visits the camp to attempt to give a lecture on the Palestinian struggle. He doesn't get very far before he's interrupted by shouts of new demands. Hassan tells Achmed not to stand for anymore of it and the next day, when the Germans complain about their training again, Achmed acts. That night a group of fedayeen storm the Germans' quarters and disarm them.

Also, within the group, a conflict develops between Baader and Peter Homann, the man suspected of being the masked gunman who freed Baader. The two are old acquaintances but during the training they fall out drastically. Homann starts to hang out with Achmed and the fedayeen. This arouses suspicion amongst his countrymen, he's called a traitor and there's talk of a tribunal and liquidation. Finally the Palestinians have to take Homann out of the camp and give him a minder.

The PLO get Homann to write a report about the group and the political situation in the BRD, then Abu Hassan takes him for a meal and arranges a meeting with the others. Homann listens in from another room as Hassan guarantees everybody a safe passage back to Germany, and arms possibly, but ignores Gudrun Ensslin's accusation that Homann is an Israeli spy and should be shot. Gudrun also makes a peculiar request on behalf of Ulrike Meinhof: could her children be brought up in one of the Palestinian orphan camps. Hassan says sure, if that's what she wants, but she'll never see them again.

AUGUST 9: The group return to West Berlin via the East without a hitch. Peter Homann decides to go his own way, the PLO give him an Arab passport (in the name of Omar Sharif), $200 and a ticket for a flight from Beirut to Rome. He arrives in Rome a week after the others return to Berlin and gets on a train to Hamburg.

This is where 'Baader-Meinhof Group' author, Stefan Aust comes back into his own story. After the springing of Baader, Aust is commissioned by (the German) 'Panorama' to do a documentary on Ulrike Meinhof. In the course of his research he unsuccessfully tries to contact Peter Homann (who lived with Meinhof for a while in Berlin). When Homann returns from the Middle East he contacts Aust and tells him of the plans for Ulrike Meinhof's children.

After Ulrike went underground, friends had smuggled her kids through France and Italy to a hippy colony near Mount Etna. Peter

23

Homann subsequently makes contact with a woman who'd looked after them and she tells him someone is coming from Berlin to take them to Jordan. She also gives Homann the password, 'Professor Schnase' and a phone number, which Homann rings and says someone will be at Palermo airport the next day to pick up the girls. Then Aust flies down to Sicily, takes the girls off the hands of the Mount Etna hippies and returns them to their father, his old boss Klaus Rainer Röhl.

This lands Aust in hot water with the subjects of his future book. When the Berlin group call Sicily and find the children already gone, they inevitably find the woman who'd told Homann and Aust and come looking for them. Fortunately for Aust, when Baader and Mahler call on him one day, another old friend of his persuades them to let him check for police first. Aust manages to slip out the back, takes an extended holiday and goes around armed for some time after. Peter Homann eventually turns himself in (when he's no longer suspected of being the masked man) and is released after a brief spell remanded in custody.

CAR TROUBLE

HOW TO ROB A BANK - THE TRIPLE COUP - THE FIRST ARRESTS - FEDERAL REPUBLIC RECON AND THE DOUBLES METHOD

Meanwhile in Berlin preparations for the underground struggle continue. More apartments are rented, cars acquired and schili called upon to provide financial assistance. Ulrike Meinhof, in particular, excels at the latter – she knows all the prominent liberals there are to know – but apparently she isn't much good at anything else. According to Aust, the courageous journalist comes off even worse than the brilliant lawyer Mahler when confronted with the wrath of Baader and Ensslin. (Her importance in the group isn't anything like the 'Baader-Meinhof' moniker suggests.)

New recruits are forthcoming too, and Hans-Jürgen Bäcker makes an especially important contact when he recruits two motor mechanics, Karl-Heinz Ruhland and Eric Grusdat. Bäcker introduces them to Horst Mahler and, through a combination of political conviction and financial incentive, they agree to doctor stolen cars – changing serial and registration numbers, re-sprays and so forth – but they are soon to get more direcly involved.

EARLY SEPTEMBER: Horst Mahler tells Ruhland and Grusdat that the group plans to rob four banks simultaneously and asks if they want in. They say they do and Grusdat devises a 'crow's foot' tack to immobilise any police cars that might pursue their getaway cars.

SEPTEMBER 29: The day of the raids: Gudrun Ensslin's group find that their bank, in Siemenstr. is swarming with building workers. So Mahler, who's co-ordinating, tells the Ensslin group to join his (Baader/Goergens/Proll/Grusdat). Then Ruhland and Grusdat are driven by Bäcker to the building next to to the Berliner bank in Rheinstr. Mahler is already there, complaining that his synchronised watch has let him down and they're 10 minutes early. Baader and the

The Concept of the Urban Guerrilla

'If we are correct in saying that American imperialism is a paper tiger, ie that it can ultimately be defeated, and if the Chinese Communists are correct in their thesis that victory over American imperialism has become possible because the struggle against it is now being waged in all four corners of the earth, with the result that the forces of imperialism are fragmented, a fragmentation which makes them possible to defeat – if this is correct then there is no reason to exclude or disqualify any particular country or any particular region from taking part in the anti-imperialist struggle because the forces of revolution are especially weak there and the forces of reaction especially strong.As it is wrong to discourage the forces of revolution by underestimating their power, so it is wrong to suggest they should seek confrontations in which these forces cannot but be squandered or annihilated. The contradiction between the sincere comrades in the organisations – let's forget about the prattlers – and the Red Army Fraction, is that we charge them with discouraging the forces of revolution and they suspect us of squandering the forces of revolution. Certainly, this analysis does indicate the directions in which the fraction of those comrades working in the factories and at local level and the Red Army Fraction are overdoing things, if they are overdoing things. Dogmatism and adventurism have since time immemorial been characteristic deviations in periods of revolutionary weakness in all countries. Anarchists having since time immemorial been the sharpest critics of opportunism, anyone criticizing the opportunists exposes himself to the charge of anarchism. This is something of an old chestnut.

The concept of the "urban guerrilla" originated in Latin America. Here, the urban guerrilla can only be what he is there: the only revolutionary method of intervention available to what are on the whole weak revolutionary forces.

The urban guerrilla starts by recognizing that there will be no Prussian order of march of the kind in which many so-called revolutionaries would like to lead the people into battle. He starts by recognizing that by the time the moment for armed struggle arrives, it will already be too late to start preparing for it; that in a country whose potential for violence is as

Meinhof protegee, Goergens arrive next. They all get out their balaclavas and guns. Mahler gives the go-ahead and they storm into the bank.

Once inside Mahler shouts "This is a stick up! Hands up and keep quiet. After all it's not your money." Baader and Goergens jump the counter, waving the clerks out of the way with their guns. When their suitcases are sufficiently stuffed full of money they jump back over, Mahler drops a smoke-bomb and they all withdraw to the building next door and get out the back. The raid takes just three minutes.

The other two raids also go off successfully. The Mahler group take the most, DM154,182; the second DM55,152 from the Savings bank in Süd-westkorso; but Ulrike Meinhof's group only manages DM8,134 from the Savings bank in Altonauerstr, overlooking a carton containing DM95,000. Poor old Ulrike comes in for more criticism for this expensive oversight.

OCTOBER 6: A week after the 'Triple Coup' everyone meets in the Kurfürstenstr. apartment of new members, Jan-Carl Raspe and Marianne Herzog. Bäcker and Ali Jansen, another newcomer, have been to Munsterlager to see if it's possible to break into an army arsenal. They think it is and a raid is planned for mid-October. OCTOBER 8: Ulrike Meinhof and Jansen, who are to organise the raid, leave Berlin for West Germany. The same day the Popo receive a tip-off that Baader, Mahler and Ensslin will be meeting at an apartment in the name of 'Hübner' at 89 Knesebeckstr.

The police put the building under surveillance but there's no incoming or outgoing all afternoon, so they move in at 5.30. There's no answer at the door either, but a woman is spotted at the window. The door is forced and the woman confronted in the hallway. She produces ID but by then the police have found a Lima 9mm pistol, molotovs, various inflammable chemicals and some car number plates.

The woman, who turns out to be Ingrid Schubert, is searched and found to have a loaded gun on her person. She's arrested and taken away, then the police turn the record player on and make themselves comfortable. After a short while the doorbell rings. The police cautiously open the door and Horst Mahler steps into the apartment to find 12 policemen pointing their guns at him.

Apparently Horst is dressed in a ridiculous disguise and one of the police says, "Do you still think we don't recognise you, Herr Mahler?" To which Mahler gives a theatrical bow and replies, "My compliments, gentlemen." He's also found to have a loaded gun on him. Half-an-hour later, after Horst has joined Ingrid Schubert in the cells, another woman is spotted listening at the door of the Hübner apartment. One of the policemen opens the door and pulls Monika Berberich inside.

A few minutes later the bell rings again. Monika Berberich tries to shout out but several policemen jump on her. Guns at the ready, the door is opened and the police find themselves facing the elderly next door neighbour, who has come to complain about the noise. But before the number of reporters gathered outside gives the game away, Brigitte Asdonk and Irene Goergens also walk into the trap.

OCTOBER 10: The survivors of the Hübner bust meet at Kurfürstenstr. and Baader takes control. Everybody agrees that Mahler was betrayed and the finger of suspicion soon points at Hans-Jürgen Bäcker. Bäcker knew all about the meeting at Knesebeckstr. but excused himself from it. He's regarded as untrustworthy anyway; another one who doesn't get on with Baader, not fully accepting his authority. In due course he arrives to face the music, and when he storms out again the others see it as an admission of guilt and swear vengeance. Astrid Proll later claims that she shot at him from a car but missed.

Next on the agenda is how to free Horst. Grusdat has already drawn up diagrams for a mini-helicopter and plans to land it in the prison exercise yard and fly Mahler and co out. He actually begins building it but his plan is never to be put into action. Meanwhile Grusdat's partner, 'Kali' Ruhland is sent off to join Ulrike Meinhof in West Germany.

NOVEMBER 1: Ruhland meets Meinhof, who is called 'Anna' or 'Rana' within the group, at Hannover train station and the two begin a reconnaissance tour of the BRD. 'Kali' and 'Rana' visit schili in Hannover, Cologne and Oldenburg, finding safe houses for the whole group. In great and whose revolutionary traditions are as broken and feeble as the Federal Republic's, there will not – without revolutionary initiative – even be a revolutionary orientation when conditions for revolutionary struggle are better than they are at present – which will happen as an inevitable consequence of the development of late capitalism itself.

To this extent, the "urban guerrilla" is the logical consequence of the negation of parliamentary democracy long since perpetrated by its very own representatives; the only and inevitable response to emergency laws and the rule of the hand grenade; the readiness to fight with those same means the system has chosen to use in trying to eliminate its opponents. The "urban guerrilla" is based on a recognition of the facts instead of an apologia of the facts.

The student movement, for one, realized something of what the urban guerrilla can do. He can make concrete the agitation and propaganda which remain the sum total of left-wing activity. One can imagine the concept being applied to the Springer Campaign at that time or to the Heidelberg students' Cabora Bassa Campaign, to the squads in Frankfurt, or in relation to the Federal Republic's military aid to the *comprador* regimes in Africa, in relation to criticism of prison sentences and class justice, of safety legislation at work and injustice there.

The urban guerrilla can concretize verbal internationalism as the requisition of guns and money. He can blunt the state's weapon of a ban on communists by organizing an underground beyond the reach of the police. The urban guerrilla is a weapon in the class war.

The "urban guerrilla" signifies armed struggle, necessary to the extent that it is the police which make indiscriminate use of firearms, exonerating class justice from guilt and burying our comrades alive unless we prevent them. To be an "urban guerrilla" means not to let oneself be demoralized by the violence of the system.

The urban guerrilla's aim is to attack the state's apparatus of control at certain points and put them out of action, to destroy the myth of the system's omnipresence and invulnerability.

The "urban guerrilla" presupposes the organization of an illegal apparatus, in other words apartments, weapons, ammunition, cars and papers. A detailed description of what is

Oberhausen they meet a very drunk Ali Jansen in the station bar. So drunk in fact he can barely speak. Ruhland and Meinhof get him into their car and take him to Cologne. Jansen was supposed to have been getting them fresh ID but he's spent the money set aside for this purpose in the bar.

However the three of them do manage to get into the Munsterlager arms depot, and it just remains for reinforcements to arrive from Berlin before the raid proper. Then Jansen gets drunk again and leaves a radio producer's Volkswagen 'somewhat the worse for wear' (as Ulrike tells the producer afterwards). Ruhland, the mechanic, gets so upset at the sight of the wreck that he punches Jansen in the face. Then orders come from Berlin that they're to get passports and cars first, so they set off again in search of suitable municipal buildings and more vehicles.

By now the group has car theft down to a fine art, with what is called the 'Doubles Method' – Someone waits in a car park outside an apartment block, until the desired type of car comes along, usually Mercedes, because they're the easiest to hot-wire. Then the owner is followed up to his/her apartment and a few days later someone returns with opinion poll ID and asks for details of the desired vehicle. Next a new log book is forged and another car with the same technical data located. This car is stolen and fitted out with the registration and number plates of the first car. So there's two identical cars driving around and if one of the 'Doubles' is stopped and the police check up with the license bureau, they'll find the car really is registered in the name the documents say it is. (Later the Doubles Method is simplified to listening into details reported on police radio.)

NOVEMBER 15: Ruhland, Meinhof and Jansen break into Neustadt town hall and help themselves to blank passports, ID cards, official seals and notepaper. These are all posted back to Berlin, but Ulrike makes a mistake decoding the address and the stuff ends up in the Bamberg sorting office. So they have to do it all again. This time they move south to Langgöns, near Frankfurt and net 166 blank ID cards, official seals and a passport punch.

A few days after the Langgöns raid, Jan-Carl Raspe ('Fred') arrives in Polle. Meinhof and Ruhland go to pick up his car and Meinhof almost gets herself arrested – The police have the car under surveillance and approach her as she gets into it. Her papers check out okay but she panics and tries to run. That isn't enough to arrest her for – the police eventually let her go – but her picture on wanted posters throughout West Germany should have been.

The arrival of Raspe also causes personal problems amongst the recon. group. Raspe, an SDS and Kommune 1 veteran, soon ousts Ruhland from Ulrike's favours. Raspe and Meinhof leave Ruhland behind in Polle when they drive north to Bremen, then all three go to look at banks in Oberhausen. Arms are finally acquired in Frankfurt from Al Fatah reps. Ulrike Meinhof buys 23 9mm Firebirds for DM450. Raspe and Ruhland take one each, 5 are left in a Frankfurt safehouse and the rest are mailed in two parcels to Berlin.

The bungalow they've been staying at in Polle is now abandoned in favour of the Frankfurt safehouse, a journalist's apartment. And more safehouses have to be found for the others now on their way from Berlin. Baader has already sent Ulrich Scholze and Teeny Stachowiak to Nuremberg to case banks. Holger Meins, an underground film-maker who has joined the group because of increasing police harassment, and his protegee Beate Sturm go direct to Frankfurt. Ulrike Meinhof rents another bungalow in the country and finds a writer, who she doesn't know but persuades him to put up Scholze, Stachowiak, Astrid Proll, Marianne Herzog and Petra Schelm.

DECEMBER 12: Baader and Ensslin arrive in Frankfurt.

DECEMBER 15: Along with the advance party and Meins and Sturm, they take up residence at the Bad Kissingen sanatorium, a massive but dilapidated place known to more schili friends of Meinhof. After a few days there everyone moves on to prepare for more bank raids in the Ruhr.

DECEMBER 20: Ruhland is driving Beate Sturm, Ali Jansen and a involved is to be found in Marighella's *Minimanual for the Urban Guerrilla*. As for what else is involved, we are ready at any time to inform anyone who needs to know because he intends to do it. We do not know a great deal yet, but we do know something.

What is important is that one should have had some political experience in legality before deciding to take up armed struggle. Those who have joined the revolutionary left just to be trendy had better be careful not to involve themselves in something from which there is no going back.

The Red Army Fraction and the "urban guerrilla" are that fraction and praxis which, because they draw a clear dividing line between themselves and the enemy, are combatted most intensively. This presupposes a political identity, presupposes that one or two lessons have already been learned.

In our original concept, we planned to combine urban guerrilla activity with grass-roots work. What we wanted was for each of us to work simultaneously within existing socialist groups at the work place and in local districts, helping to influence the discussion process, learning, gaining experience. It has become clear that this cannot be done. These groups are under such close surveillance by the political police, their meetings, timetables, and the content of their discussions so well monitored, that it is impossible to attend without being put under surveillance oneself. We have learned that individuals cannot combine legal and illegal activity.

Becoming an "urban guerrilla" presupposes that one is clear about one's own motivation, that one is sure of being immune to "Bild-Zeitung" methods, sure that the whole anti-Semite-criminal-subhuman-murderer-arsonist syndrome they use against revolutionaries, all that shit that they alone are able to abstract and articulate and that still influences some comrades' attitudes to us, that none of this has any effect on us.

RAF

**A hundred flowers have bloomed,
They are one hundred armed revolutionary groups!'**

**Rote Armee Fraktion (RAF),
Das Konzept Stadtguerilla, April 1971**

friend of Jansen's through Oberhausen looking for cars, when they're stopped by police. Unusually there's something wrong with Ruhland's papers and he takes the opportunity to give himself up. He makes sure that the others have a chance to get away first, but it isn't long before he starts talking.

That night his erstwhile partner, Ulrike Meinhof bolts at another police checkpoint, leaving a new blonde haired picture of herself for the wanted posters. After the arrest of Ruhland all the Frankfurt apartments are raided, but by now the group's attention has moved to Nuremberg. Uli Scholze and Astrid Proll go ahead on recon, then Ulrike Meinhof and Ali Jansen join them. Late one night the four of them are attempting to steal a Mercedes. They manage to get it started but it backfires and wakes its owner, who calls the police. Meinhof and Proll get away but Scholze and Jansen's car is followed and stopped by plain-clothes police. Uli Scholze goes quietly, but Ali Jansen goes for his gun as he's being frisked. He manages to get a shot off, the plain-clothes men dive for cover and Jansen gets into their car -- but he can't get it started and when he looks up the guns are turned on him.

The rough treatment he then receives is actually acknowledged in court but he still goes down for ten years for attempted murder. Uli Scholze, on the other hand, is freed the next day and goes back to his mother and college.

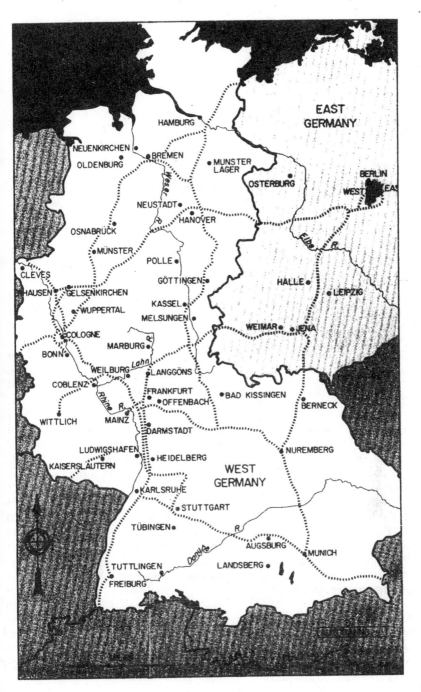

NEW TRAFFIC REGULATIONS

1970/71: THE URBAN GUERRILLA CONCEPT AND THE SPK: KILL KILL KILL FOR MENTAL HEALTH AND INNER PEACE

LATE 1970: Federal Interior Minister Genscher persuades the various Länder ministers to bring the 'Baader-Meinhof' investigation under the jurisdiction of the BKA (Bundeskriminalamt – Federal Criminal Investigation Office). Alfred Klaus of the BKA is chosen to set up a special commission on terrorism and moves into a suite of offices in the Bonn Security Group building. There he writes a 60 page preliminary report, covering the history of the group from the time of the Frankfurt firebombings.

At the same time Horst Mahler is also writing about the group from his prison cell. However his 'Statement of Position', published under the title 'New Traffic Regulations', doesn't receive the approval of those still at large. In fact they disown it completely and cross Horst off their rescue list. Ulrike Meinhof is subsequently given the job of writing a manifesto.

Meinhof's 'Urban Guerrilla Concept' is the first communique since the freeing of Baader and the first time the group go under the 'RED ARMY FACTION' ('Rote Armee Fraction') moniker. The front cover bears the now famous 'RAF' initials over a drawing of a Kalashnikov submachine gun. The name is chosen more as a joke than anything, because of what the original (British) RAF and (Russian) Red Army did to the original German Nazis.

JANUARY 1971: After casing two banks in Kassel (Astrid Proll's home town) Beate Sturm calls her parents and returns home while she still can.
JANUARY 15: The two Kassel banks are raided; final takings DM114,715.

FEBRUARY 2: Hans-Jürgen Bäcker is arrested.

FEBRUARY 10: Astrid Proll and Manfred Grashof are followed out of a Frankfurt restaurant by Michael Grünhagen, a counter-intelligence man who has already been exposed in the Berlin underground paper 'AGIT 883'. In turn, Grünhagen is being followed by Det. Chief Supt. Heinz Simons of the Bonn Security Group. In due course, Simons and Grünhagen stop Proll and Grashof and ask to see their papers. Thereupon Grashof pulls out a gun and yells at Proll, "Get out of here, run for it!" Both Proll and Grashof get away in the end, the latter thanks to a sympathetic passer-by who steers him clear of the danger-zone and buys him a U-bahn ticket. Proll is unarmed and Grashof doesn't fire his gun even when Simons shoots at him.

However, when Astrid Proll is captured in Hamburg on May 6, this incident is made into an attempted murder charge. And it's not until her second trial that it's finally dropped. (After her first trial she's released on health grounds and absconds to London, where she's eventually hounded down by the press and extradited.) Fortunately for Astrid, Federal counter-intelligence people are also at the scene and file a memo saying she didn't shoot.

Immediately after the incident the biggest manhunt so far begins. Apartments that

Astrid Proll at the time of her second trial

Ruhland named are raided in Gelsenkirchen, Frankfurt, Hamburg and Bremen. The schili have a pretty hard time of it, and the press get in on the act and many an innocent Baader/Meinhof lookalike is pulled in. Meanwhile, back in Berlin, Horst Mahler, Irene Goergens and Ingrid Schubert go on trial for their part in the Baader rescue. After two months Goergens and Schubert are found guilty of being accessories and get 6 and 4 years youth custody respectively. Horst Mahler is found not guilty but held under 'Paragraph 129' (membership of an illegal organisation) because he still has a few more charges to go.

Meanwhile, in the wake of all the RAF publicity, another far-left group appears on the scene. The 'Socialist Patients' Collective' declare in Patients Info #1: 'The system has made us sick. Let us strike the death blow to the sick system!' Founded in February 1970 by Dr. Wolfgang Huber of Heidelberg University, the SPK begins when Huber is reprimanded for refusing to co-operate with the rest of the psychiatric department. This leads to a protest by Huber's group-therapy patients. Huber is subsequently sacked and mobilises his patients to occupy the administration offices of the university. While the patients go on hunger strike, Huber warns the director that some of them might commit suicide. The director gives way, reinstates Huber on full pay and gives him 4 rooms for a year.

The subsequent SPK 'working circles' are officially: Dialectics, Marxism, Sexuality, Education and Religion. Unofficially they are: Explosives, Radio Transmission (listening into police radio), Photography (compiling photos of all personnel, premises, etc of the Heidelberg police), Judo and Karate. A 'mentally ill' girl who is sent to Dr. Huber for treatment is returned to her parents after two weeks, because 'she has made no noticeable political progress'.

MID-FEBRUARY 1971: SPK members Siegfried Hausner and Carmen Roll attempt to bomb the BRD president's train. But by the time Roll gets to Heidelberg station with the bomb, the train has gone.

SPRING 1971: The SPK begins to arm itself and link up with the RAF, making SPK members available to bolster the RAF's dwindling ranks. Thus a 'Second Generation' RAF is formed by SPK members Gerhard Müller, Elisabeth von Dyck, Knut Folkerts, Ralf Baptist Friedrich, Siegfried Hausner, Sieglinde Hofmann, Klaus Jünschke, Bernhard

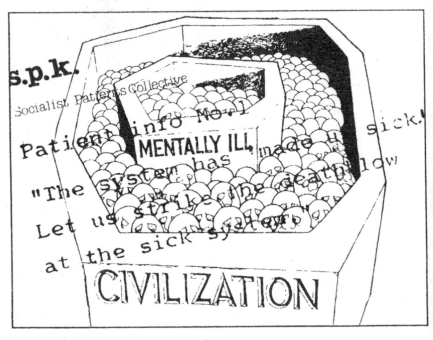

Rössner, Carmen Roll, Margrit Schiller and Lutz Taufer. Simultaneously there are still members of the SPK who think they are receiving self-help therapy.

JUNE 24: A group of SPK members (believed to include Ralf Reinders and Alfred Mahrlander) are stopped by police in Wiesental, near Dr. Huber's home. There's a car chase and some shooting. One of the policemen takes a bullet in the arm. After this there's a massive round-up of the SPK, including Dr. Huber and his wife. The ones that get away go underground and join the RAF. In Patients Info #51 every 'SPK' is replaced by 'RAF'. The following month the SPK announces its dissolution and becomes 'IZRU' (Information Zentrum Rote Volks-Universität), proposing the formation of guerrilla cells. By this time the original autonomous collective has been replaced by an inner-circle of about 12, who constitute the political leadership of anything up to 500 'patients'.

THE WAR OF THE SIX AGAINST THE SIX MILLION

JUNE 2 MOVEMENT - THE DEATH OF PETRA SCHELM - THE CHIEF COMMISSIONER AND HIS SECRET COMPUTER WORLD - AND A BUCKET OF TAR IN THE KISSER

JULY 8: Tommy Weisbecker and Georg von Rauch are tried for assaulting a journalist from the Springer magazine 'Quick'. Georg is convicted but Tommy acquitted. However the court manages to mix them up, so Georg escapes and goes underground and Tommy has to be released when he reveals that he's not Georg.

Shortly after this the 'JUNE 2 MOVEMENT' is formed, as a sort of anarcho-situationist alternative to the RAF. When former K1 member, Bommi Baumann takes the J2M helm on his release from jail, Baader and Ensslin ask them to join the RAF in Hamburg. But Baumann turns down their offer, preferring to stay in Berlin and concentrate on springing people from prison.

JULY 15: 3,000 police cordon off main roads all over the BRD to carry out traffic checks for wanted RAF members. In the afternoon a BMW ('Baader-Meinhof-Wagen') breaks through one of the 15 roadblocks around Hamburg. A police Mercedes takes chase and manages to force the BMW off the road. The occupants, Werner Hoppe and Petra Schelm run off in different directions.

Hoppe is followed by a helicopter and surrenders, surrounded by 80 or so police. But Petra Schelm doesn't surrender. The accounts of her fate vary quite drastically but, whether she goes out in a hail of bullets 'Bonnie and Clyde' style ('Hitler's Children') or by a single bullet from a police marksmen ('Baader-Meinhof Group'), the end result is the same: 19 year old Petra Schelm is the first casualty in the 'war of the six against the six million'.

JULY 20: Dieter Kunzelmann is arrested and charged with involvement in West Berlin bomb attacks. In due course he gets 9 years for attempted murder.

SEPTEMBER 1: Horst Herold becomes Chief Commissioner of the BKA, and begins to change it into a German version of the FBI. First he gets Interior Minister Genscher to approve a decentralising communication system between the BKA and regional police. Then he installs a computer centre at his Wiesbaden headquarters and meticulously learns how to use it. In the end Herold becomes so obsessed with his computer that he moves into the complex, so he can be with it all the time. Nothing is denied it, not only is it fed data on wanted persons but also defendants already on trial and 'people who represent a danger'.

In 1979 a review of Herold's system lists 37 data files containing 4.7 million names and 3,100 organisations. The fingerprint collection contains 2.1 million sets of prints. The photographic section, 1.9 million pictures. The handwriting file, 6,000 samples of writing. And there's a 'Personal ID Centre' with biographies of 3,500 people. The heart of the BKA's 'electronic memory' is the 'PIOS' (Persons/Institutions/Objects/Items) data-file. 'PIOS/Terrorism' contains 135,000 people, 5,500 institutions, 115,000 objects and 74,000 items. Not to mention the 'Contacts/Surveillance of detainees' file which lists 6,632 people who have merely visited terrorist suspects in prison.

As Horst Herold stores and processes all his data, thinking up fantastic ideas to combat all crime, not just terrorism, he alternates between omnipotence ('I could have stopped the Nazis') and despondency: during the Baader-Meinhof trial he complains that the only difference between the terrorists in their isolation block and him, in his 'own personal Stammheim', is he doesn't get any public sympathy. Over the years Herold develops a weird love/hate relationship with Andreas Baader. He's proud of the fact that Baader makes his articles on counter-terrorism required reading for new RAF recruits, and once rather predictably says, "Baader was the only man who ever really understood me, and I'm the only man who ever really understood him."

Herold also agrees with the RAF that what they're doing should be treated as political and military, not as ordinary criminal activity. However where it would lead if Herold was allowed to act on this conclusion (further than he did) doesn't bear thinking about. Herold sees himself as the man who won the 70s war against terrorism and finds any comparisons with 'Big Brother' cruelly unfair. In March 1981 he retires to a modest house in the grounds of a police barracks in southern Germany, surrounded by a fence and bullet-proof parapet. Here he whiles away the days, working out new programmes to fight crime on the computer system in the basement, only venturing out accompanied by two BKA men armed with submachine guns.

Pig ist Pig . . . Pig muß Putt

Befreit alle Gefangenen !

Liebe Hella!
Ich möchte Dir zum erstenmal schreiben.
Sei nicht böse, daß es so lange gedauert
hat, aber es hat keinen Sinn, sich nur
ein Hallo zuzurufen. Ich habe hier im
Knast gehört, daß Du wieder verhaftet
worden bist bei den Aktionen auf dem
Kudamm. Du sollst mit Steinen nach
Bullen geschmissen haben. Erinnerst Du
Dich noch daran als wir uns das erste
Mal unterhielten — es war im Zodiak und ist jetzt bald ein Jahr her. Du sagtest da-
mals, Du könntest uns nicht verstehen, daß wir jetzt bald ein Jahr her. Du sagtest da-
se Pigs etc. Jetzt gehst Du auch auf die Straße und mit Dir immer mehr Typen. Du
wirst sehen, daß es immer mehr Arbeiter oder wie in meinem Fall ausgeflippte Arbeiter werden, die für die eigenen Interessen kämpfen. Das Leben, wie es bisher abrollt,
erscheint uns sinnlos, öde, leer und unmenschlich. Wir versuchen auf irgendeine Art
auszubrechen, um Gefühle des Glücks, der Zärtlichkeit und der Gemeinsamkeit zu
erleben, die uns diese bürgerliche Gesellschaft verweigert. Die Aussicht, ein ganzes
Leben unter diesen herrschenden Verhältnissen leben und arbeiten zu müssen, erscheint
uns derart entsetzlich, daß wir uns abwenden, zum Gift greifen und vor uns hindäm-
mern ohne uns um irgendetwas noch zu kümmern. Aber bald müssen wir entdecken,
daß uns das System auch dabei nicht in Ruhe läßt. RD-Bullen werden uns auf den
Hals gejagt.
Und dann das Geldproblem. Diese vertierte Gesellschaft hat es geschafft, alles so ein-
zurichten, daß jeder gezwungen ist, mitzumachen oder in der Gosse zu verrecken.
Ich kann hier jeden Tag die Opfer dieser Unterdrückung sehen und begreife durch deren

Lebensgeschichte die Geschichte des
Kapitalismus. Solange nicht die öko-
nomischen Verhältnisse verändert
sind, solange ist ein menschliches Leben unmöglich. Es gibt nur einen Aus-
weg aus unserer Situation und der
heißt soziale Weltrevolution. Weltbür-
gerkrieg. Wir müssen anstelle der Kon-
kurrenz und des Individualismus unsere proletarische Solidarität setzen und
unsere Bedürfnisse, die sich im Kampf

June 2 Movement: A pig is a pig... The pig must be offed! Free all prisoners!

SEPTEMBER 25: Two policemen, both named Ruf but not related, are shot at as they approach a wrongly parked car on the Freiburg-Basel autobahn. One of them is seriously wounded, the other shot through the hand. They identify their assailants as Holger Meins and Margrit Schiller.

MID-OCTOBER: Baader and Ensslin return to Berlin. Plans are afoot to kidnap the American, British and French zone commanders in the biggest RAF operation to date. But first Baader and Ensslin agree to help in an attempt to spring Irene Goergens and Ingrid Schubert (as long as they rejoin the RAF and not J2M). Baader suggests an anti-aircraft gun bombardment of the Ruhleben police barracks as a diversion, but no one can get hold of the guns. Then the rescue attempt itself is aborted because the girls fail to saw through their prison bars.

From here on things go downhill between the RAF and J2M. Gudrun Ensslin chastises Bommi Baumann for smoking too much dope, being too promiscuous and not taking 'the Job' seriously enough. Basically it's a clash of lifestyles. Baader, on the other hand, has fallen almost entirely under the influence of speed, chain-smoking Gitanes and drinking excessive amounts of coffee. After the inevitable RAF/J2M bust-up Baader and Ensslin link up with Brigitte Mohnhaupt and their accommodation is provided by old acquaintances from the student days, Katharina Hammerschmidt and Edelgard G.

During subsequent police raids Edelgard G. turns herself in and is told she will never see her child again unless she talks. After 3 weeks she makes a statement and is set free. A few months later the German Press Agency receives a picture of a woman covered in tar. Attached to it is a note saying: 'This is Edelgaard G., an informer who is hand in glove with the killer pigs. Long live the RAF!' Despite further questioning by the police, Edelgaard G. doesn't make any more statements.

Katharina Hammerschmidt comes off even worse. She eventually gives herself up after being on the run for some time. In prison she develops a tumour, which prison doctors fail to notice. Before outside help is allowed in, it turns malignant and she dies.

We Rob Banks! *International Times*, February 1972

A KIND OF REVOLUTIONARY FICTION

1971/72: ORDER OF DEATH - THE KILLING OF GEORG VON RAUCH AND TOMMY WEISBECKER - THE PRIMACY OF PRAXIS AND THE MAY BOMBINGS

OCTOBER 22: Another shootout in Hamburg. This time the police suffer a casualty. Margrit Schiller is being chased by two policemen, when two other RAF members (identified as Irmgard Möller and Gerhard Müller) come to her assistance. In the ensuing gun battle one of the policemen, Norbert Schmid is hit four times and dies on his way to hospital.

OCTOBER 23: Margrit Schiller, who still gets caught, is somewhat gratuitously displayed to press photographers; and ends up getting 2 years. A reward of DM10,000 is offered for information leading to the capture of the others.

OCTOBER 25: The apartment of a pop singer, away on tour, is raided in the neighbouring Poppenbüttel district of Hamburg. There are signs that it has been recently vacated along with RAF paraphernalia, explosives, thousands of bullets, detonators, walkie-talkies, police uniforms and a list of 'progressive pastors to be asked for assistance'.

NOVEMBER: A parcel labelled 'Glass – Handle with care', sent from a town near Hamburg to a Berlin pottery, comes open in the mail and bullets fall out. Police find six other parcels awaiting collection at the pottery containing: 16 Firebird and Parabellum pistols, three automatic rifles, silencers and sights, thousands of cartridges, explosives and detonators, walkie-talkies, wigs and beards, number plates, car ignition locks, you name it.

DECEMBER 3: As the Berlin police step up the RAF/J2M hunt, border checks intensify and everybody from estate agents to key cutters are asked to co-operate. Marianne Herzog and Rolf Pohle arrested as a result.

DECEMBER 4: A stolen Ford Transit and a Volkswagen are stopped in Eisenacherstr. One of the occupants of the two vehicles does a runner, the other three are lined up against a wall with their hands above their heads. Georg von Rauch goes for his gun and is shot dead on the spot. In the ensuing chaos Bommi Baumann gets away, losing his pursuers by joining a group of Hare Krishnas on the Ku-damm and getting some of his teenage girlfriends to walk him through the police checkpoints.
DECEMBER 5: 7,000 take to the streets in protest at the von Rauch killing.

LATE DECEMBER: RAF hardcore move back to West Germany to usher in the new year with a bombing campaign. Frankfurt, once again becomes the eye of the storm. Just before Christmas, Holger Meins visits the metal sculptor Dierk Hoff and tells him he's working on a film which needs technical assistance. Hoff asks what the film is about and Meins replies, "It's a kind of revolutionary fiction." He agrees to help anyway, and Meins gets him to reproduce a grenade casing and a bomb mould which could be attached to a corset: Hoff is told this is for the final scene, where a woman pretends to be pregnant so she can plant a bomb in a toilet. Hoff has his doubts but he gets in too deep and has to continue producing more and more realistic props.
DECEMBER 22: During a bank raid in Kaiserslautern the police suffer another casualty. The raid is later accredited to the former SPK member Klaus Jünschke, Ingeborg Barz and Wolfgang Grundmann, but at the time there is nothing to connect it directly to the RAF. Nonetheless, the press (namely the Springer papers) use the incident to whip up further Baader-Meinhof fear and loathing. The takings of the raid are DM133,987.
JANUARY 1972: A Cologne police sergeant nearly nets the biggest fish of them all/gets himself killed, when he decides to check out the driver of a BMW with Berlin plates. When the driver winds down his window, the sergeant points the barrel of his gun at him and asks to see his papers. But instead of papers, Andreas Baader produces a longer barrelled pistol. The sergeant swerves out of the way as Baader fires and speeds away.
FEBRUARY: A J2M bomb explodes at the British Yacht Club in West Berlin; a gesture of solidarity with the IRA which kills a 66 year old German boatbuilder.
FEBRUARY 21: 8 RAF members in carnival masks raid the Ludwigshafen Mortgage and Exchange Bank and make off with DM285,000. Ingeborg Barz subsequently calls home but she never makes it. In July 1973 her decomposed body is found near Munich by the autobahn. Police claim to have information (from Gerhard Müller) that Baader executed her because she wanted to quit the RAF.
MARCH 1: Richard Epple, a 17 year old apprentice is mowed down by a

police submachine gun after a car chase through Tübingen. The reason he didn't stop: Richard Epple was driving without a licence.

MARCH 2: After a tip-off, Tommy Weisbecker and Carmen Roll are seen leaving an apartment in Augsberg. They are followed to a hotel, outside which Tommy is shot dead before he has a chance to produce his ID/gun (depending on which story you believe). Carmen Roll is arrested shortly afterwards. Two weeks later she's administered a near lethal dose of Ether by prison doctors.

On the same day as the Weisbecker killing, in Hamburg, police occupy an apartment where a RAF forgery workshop has been discovered. After dark, Manfred Grashof and Wolfgang Grundmann walk into the apartment. The police are quicker on the draw once more. Grundmann puts his hands up but Grashof returns fire. A superintendent and Grashof take two bullets apiece. The policeman dies two weeks later. But Grashof survives, only to be removed from hospital and put in an isolation cell with the lights on day and night.

MARCH 15: Karl-Heinz Ruhland gets four and a half years.

MARCH 29: Till Meyer of J2M is arrested in Bielefeld after another shoot out. No casualties this time.

APRIL 19: 400 police raid the '(Georg von) Rauch Haus' in Kreuzberg. 27 apprentices are taken away for questioning, but J2M members in residence successfully make themselves scarce.

Bomb damage to the officers' mess of the US Army Headquarters, Frankfurt, May 1972

The Primacy of Praxis:

Whether it is right to organise armed resistance now depends on whether it is possible. This can only be ascertained in practice.'

MAY: USAF mine harbours in North Vietnam. Series of bombings in West Berlin in protest.

MAY 11: Three pipe-bombs go off in the entrance and officers' mess of the 5th US Army Corps stationed at the IG Farben building in Frankfurt. 13 American soldiers are injured and Lt. Col. Paul Bloomquist, veteran of two tours of Vietnam, is killed by a shard of glass which gets him in the throat. Estimated damage to the IG Farben building: DM1 million. RAF Communique #1, claiming responsibility for the 'Petra Schelm Commando':

'West Berlin and West Germany will no longer be a safe hinterland for the strategists of extermination in Vietnam. They must know that their crimes against the Vietnamese people have made them new and bitter enemies, that there will be nowhere in the world left where they can be safe from the attacks of revolutionary guerrilla units... WE DEMAND THE IMMEDIATE END OF THE MINE BLOCKADE OF NORTH VIETNAM... WE DEMAND THE COMPLETE WITHDRAWAL OF AMERICAN TROOPS FROM INDOCHINA...VICTORY TO THE VIET-CONG!'

Bomb damage in the parking lot of the US Army headqarters in Heidelberg, May 1972

MAY 12: Two explosive devices go off in the Augsburg police headquarters. 5 policemen are injured. The same day, in Munich, a car bomb is detonated in the car park of the State Criminal Investigation Office. 60 cars are destroyed along with most of the building's windows. RAF Communique #2 claims responsibility for both bombings in the name of the 'Tommy Weisbecker Commando'.

MAY 15: A red Volkswagen, containing Frau Gerta Buddenberg, explodes in Karlsruhe. She is the wife of Judge Wolfgang Buddenberg, the judge responsible for most of the RAF arrest warrants and for moving Manfred Grashof from hospital to the isolation cell. Frau Buddenberg isn't killed but left crippled by the bomb which was intended for her husband. RAF Communique #3, claiming responsibility for the 'Manfred Grashof Commando', is the first of many attacks on the 'isolation torture' RAF prisoners are forced to endure.

MAY 19: Two bombs explode in the Springer building on Kaiser-Wilhelmstr. Hamburg. Three other bombs in the building fail to go off and three telephone warnings are ignored, bomb threats being quite a common occurrence at Springer concerns. In all 17 people are injured. RAF Communique #4 (for 'June 2 Commando'):

> 'Springer would rather risk seeing his workers and clerical staff injured by bombs than risk losing a few hours' working time, which means profit, over a false alarm. To capitalists, profit is everything and the people who create it are dirt. We are deeply upset to hear that workers and clerical staff were injured.'

MAY 24: Two car bombs explode within 15 seconds of each other outside a barracks and mess hall at the European headquarters of the US Army in Heidelberg. A Vietnam Vet. Captain and two Sergeants are killed (one by a Coca-cola machine falling on top of him) and five more GIs wounded. RAF Communique #5, claiming responsibility for 'July 15 Commando' (date of Petra Schelm's killing):

> 'On Monday, the foreign minister in Hanoi again accused the USA of bombarding densely populated areas in North Vietnam. In the last 7 weeks the USAF has dropped more bombs over Vietnam than were dropped over Germany and Japan together in the whole of the Second World War. The Pentagon is trying to stop the North Vietnamese offensive with more than a million bombs. This is Genocide, Murder of the People, Annihilation, Auschwitz.'

CAPTURE 9

THE FRANKFURT GARAGE SIEGE - BLACK SEPTEMBER - A CLEAR AWARENESS THAT YOUR CHANCE OF SURVIVAL IS NIL - RED AID - AND THE GUN SPEAKS

MAY 29: Horst Herold calls together the leaders of all the regional commissions to announce a nationwide sweep-search on May 31. 'Operation Watersplash' is to involve the entire BRD police force, but when Herold's big break comes it isn't as a result of the search; it comes in the form of an anonymous tip-off that young people in big cars are bringing gas cylinders to a garage in the Hofeckweg district of Frankfurt. BKA men locate the garage and check it out. Substances they find which are confirmed to be explosives are replaced by bonemeal and the garage staked out.

JUNE 1: 5.50am. A Porsche Targa pulls up outside the garage and three men get out. Two of the men, Holger Meins and Andreas Baader go into the garage, the third man, Jan-Carl Raspe stays outside by the car and soon becomes aware that he is not alone. In fact police are swarming all over the place. Then Jillian Becker ('Hitler's Children') predictably claims Raspe tries to leg it; but Stefan Aust has a squad car approaching him first, Raspe drawing his gun and two more policemen rushing him. Then Raspe takes flight firing off a shot, only to be captured in a nearby garden. (At the same time, a male nurse on his way to work, is also pounced upon and arrested before he can explain who he is.) .

Following Raspe's arrest, a surveillance car is pushed up against the garage doors and Baader fires a shot through the side. Then holes are knocked through the thick glass panels at the back of the garage. At this point, Baader and Meins are laughing and waving their guns at the police. Next tear gas grenades are shot through the holes and the top BKA man at the scene tells them to throw out their guns, take off their outer clothing and come out with their hands up. Baader and Meins push one side of the doors out and the police, thinking they're about to surrender, remove the car. Thereupon, Baader flings the tear gas grenades back at the police.

7.45am. An armoured car is driven into the garage doors and more tear gas fired into the garage. Then Det. Sgt. Bernhard Honke gets access to an overlooking apartment, gets Baader in his sights and shoots him in the leg. Shortly after that, Holger Meins comes out with his hands up; he's ordered to strip to his underpants, then he walks towards the police line.

Holger Meins arrested, Frankfurt, June 1972

Ten minutes later, the armoured car goes in again, this time supported by police in bullet-proof vests. They find Andreas Baader, hair dyed with peroxide, lying bleeding still clutching his gun. One of the policemen kicks it out of his hand then four of them drag him away, still struggling, on a stretcher. These events are relayed live across the BRD by a Frankfurt TV crew, who stopped off on their way to a race track.

After the arrest of Baader, Meins and Raspe, Gudrun Ensslin joins Ulrike Meinhof, Klaus Jünschke and Gerhard Müller in Hamburg. Spirits are understandably low, as Jünschke puts it, "It was like going downhill out of control, if you jump out you're done for, if you carry on you're done for just the same."

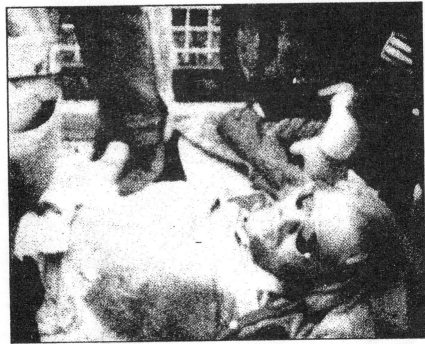

Andreas Baader arrested, Frankfurt, June 1972

JUNE 7: Ensslin is being driven through Hamburg by Jünschke. She thinks he's driving erratically, so they switch to a taxi. Then the taxi driver looks at her suspiciously, so panicking, Gudrun goes to a boutique to buy new clothes. While she's trying something on, a sales girl moves her jacket and sees her gun. The manageress subsequently calls the police and delays her until they arrive. Thereupon, Gudrun makes calmly for the door but gets grabbed before she reaches it. A desperate struggle ensues and two policemen end up on the ground, before Gudrun Ensslin is finally overpowered.

> Police report of apartment search (key to which found on Gudrun Ensslin at time of her arrest) 'Re: Hunt for violent anarchist criminals. Subject: Conspirators' apartment at 71 Seidenstr. Stuttgart. Attached: 22 Mickey Mouse comic books were found in the above mentioned apartment. There are good grounds for suspecting that these Mickey Mouse books were read by the gang member Andreas Baader.'

JUNE 9: Brigitte Mohnhaupt and Bernhard Braun (SPK/J2M) are arrested in Berlin.
JUNE 15: The schili finally turn on and turn in Ulrike Meinhof. Fritz

Rodewald, a left-wing teacher living in Hannover is asked to put up two people, who turn out to be Ulrike Meinhof and Gerhard Müller. He agrees but has second thoughts and calls the police. (True to trendy lefty form, he later donates the reward money to the RAF defence fund.)

Not long after plain clothes police arrive at the building, Gerhard Müller goes out to make a phone call and is promptly nabbed. Reinforcements are called but there's to be no repeat of the Frankfurt siege. Ulrike Meinhof is arrested without much of a struggle, when she answers the door to the apartment. However once she's captured Ulrike causes quite a commotion and struggles for hours; hence the unflattering, swollen faced pictures that will be used for posterity. To give Andreas Baader his due, he still looks cool in dark glasses and peroxide hair when he's dragged out of the garage.

JUNE 25: Police raid another apartment in Stuttgart and Scottish ex-pat Ian MacLeod is shot dead. Nothing but the most tenuous rumours link MacLeod with the RAF. He's merely an unfortunate statistic on Herold's computer whose apartment may or may not have been used by the group.

JULY 7: Klaus Jünschke and Irmgard Möller are arrested in Offenbach, after being set up by new RAF member Hans-Peter Konieczny.

SEPTEMBER 5: A 'Black September' commando unit climb the fence of the Olympic Village in Munich and shoot their way into the Israeli team quarters. Two Israeli athletes are killed and 9 more taken hostage. Then, after a day's televised bargaining, the commando unit and their hostages are driven to Fürstenfeldbruck airport. They are all to be flown to Cairo, but as the Palestinians board their plane police marksmen open fire. In the ensuing gun battle all the Israeli athletes (11 in all), one of the police and five of the Palestinians are killed; leaving three to carry the can.

RAF prisoners spend the first year of imprisonment in separate jails, isolated not only from ordinary prisoners but from each other. Ulrike Meinhof spends a year in almost complete acoustic isolation before bad publicity forces prison authorities to move her. She describes the experience as: 'The feeling that your head is exploding... The feeling of your spinal chord being pressed into your brain...Furious aggression for which there is no outlet. That's the worst thing. A clear awareness that your chance of survival is nil.'

> RAF code of conduct in jail: 'Not a word to the pigs, in whatever guise they may appear, particularly as doctors. Not a single word. And naturally we give them no assistance, never lift a finger to help them. Nothing but hostility and contempt... No provocation; that's important. But we will defend ourselves implacably, relentlessly, with what human methods we have.'

SEPTEMBER 20: Ulrike Meinhof is taken to Zweibrücken prison to take part in an identity parade. Naturally against her will. In fact, she objects so much that the other women in the parade are told to act like they're resisting. The resulting chaos, with all the women struggling and shouting "I'm Ulrike Meinhof!" makes it impossible for the witnesses to recognise the real one. Even though by now she is the most famous woman in Germany.

DECEMBER 11: Till Meyer is sentenced to 3 years for the attempted murder of a policemen.

LATE 1972: 'Red Aid', the political prisoners' support group, puts out a series of leaflets, intending to show how the RAF are being broken down and denied basic rights. However, the prisoners themselves are not impressed. Andreas Baader: 'Because our comrades are half dead, they can't think we're anything else ourselves. They're twisting the thing the same way the pigs twist it worldwide: Violence is taboo, they dig themselves in behind death like a lot of parsons... The gun livens things up. The colonialized European comes alive, not to the subject and problem of the violence of our circumstances, but because all armed action subjects the force of circumstances to the force of events... I say our book should be entitled 'THE GUN SPEAKS'.'

Around this time Baader is called by the defence at the Horst Mahler trial in Berlin to give evidence about prison conditions. Apropos this, Baader announces the first RAF hunger strike, which is to last two months. Baader's lawyer at the time, Hans-Christian Ströbele, gets the Federal Prosecutor to relax the conditions and take Ulrike Meinhof out of the 'Dead Section' at Ossendorf jail. Baader is dubious but Ströbele manages to persuade him to call off the hunger strike. No sooner has he done so than Ulrike Meinhof is back in the 'Dead Section'. Ströbele doesn't last long as Baader's brief.

FEBRUARY 1973: Margrit Schiller is released and goes back underground. RAF defence lawyers have their own token hunger strike outside the Federal Supreme Court. And Gudrun Ensslin hassles her lawyers to get Amnesty International and the like onto their case. Neither has much effect, and when Ulrike Meinhof is finally moved, after 8 months of complete acoustic isolation, it's to a cell previously occupied by a child murderer.

MARCH: 'Black September' gunmen hold American, Belgian and Jordanian diplomats hostage at the Saudi Arabian embassy in Khartoum. Their demands include the release of a 'Black September' man held in Jordan, Sirhan Sirhan. Bobby Kennedy's assassin and the RAF prisoners. When their demands aren't met they kill two American diplomats and one Belgian.

AGAINST LEVIATHAN AGAINST HISTORY

1973/74: THE RESISTANCE OF THE CELL - STAMMHEIM - THE THIRD HUNGER STRIKE - AND THE MARTYRDOM OF HOLGER MEINS

'By art is created that great Leviathan, called a Commonwealth or a State, which is but an artificial man.'
Opening sentence of Hobbes' 'Leviathan', quoted at the beginning of 'Moby Dick'.

In order to confuse the mail censors, Gudrun Ensslin gives everybody cover-names from 'Moby Dick', a RAF favourite. All the names have allegorical significance: Gudrun is the cook, 'who kept the pans well scoured and preached to the sharks'; Baader is of course 'Captain Ahab', 'who destroyed himself in the hunt for Moby Dick'; Horst Mahler is 'a prosperous retired whaler... though a sworn foe to human bloodshed yet had he, in his straight-bodied coat, spilled tons upon tons of Leviathan gore.' (Gudrun must have been in a particularly generous mood when she chose that one.)

Holger Meins became 'Starbuck', the chief mate, described in 'Moby Dick' thus: 'Starbuck's body and coerced will were Ahab's, so long as Ahab kept his magnet at Starbuck's brain; still he knew for all this the chief mate, in his soul, abhorred his captain's quest'; Jan-Carl Raspe is 'Carpenter', the multi-purpose coffin-maker for the victims of the hunt for the great white whale; Gerhard Möller, who later turns state's evidence, is 'Queequeg': 'an idolator at heart, he yet lived among these Christians, wore their clothes and tried to talk their gibberish.'

The RAF prisoners manage to keep operating as a group by way of mail to and from the 'Red Lawyers'; and maintain their dynamic force

51

with a strict 'Info-system', instigated by Gudrun Ensslin: 'If we don't make it systematic, sooner or later there'll be a balls-up and then there'll be people out of action, in jail, pious, stupid...' The RAF's idea of an order she describes thus: 'An order results from the construction of the collective and the breaking down of every kind of hierarchy. An order is something you're convinced of, or something you come to be convinced of. If that's not possible, then you're out...' When Astrid Proll fails to whole-heartedly participate in the first hunger strike, Ulrike Meinhof writes: 'I told her she'll be thrown out of the RAF... I didn't mean it as a threat, just as a fact.'

The Info-system is used as a vigorous dialectic in criticism and self-criticism. It is also used to amass voluminous libraries on how to be an urban guerrilla. Books that get past the censors include such titles as: 'The German Journal of Weaponry', 'Military Technology', 'Radio Technology', 'Small-scale Warfare Instructor', 'Urban Guerrilla Warfare', 'Special Forces Handbook' and 'The Explosives Expert'.

The RAF experiment – staking life and freedom to show the state in its true colours – is being taken a stage further. As Gudrun Ensslin puts it, to the 'Auschwitz Stage': 'The difference between the Dead Section and Isolation is the difference between Auschwitz and Buchenwald. It's a simple distinction; more people survived Buchenwald than Auschwitz. Those of us in there, to put it bluntly, can only be surprised they don't spray the gas in. Nothing else surprises us...' Ulrike Meinhof: 'When we speak of torture, all you can say is: what do you want, you're still alive.'

MAY 8 - JUNE 29: The Second Hunger Strike. This time 40 prisoners take part, including many who are not in the RAF. Prison authorities employ force-feeding for the first time. Conditions improve slightly as the hunger strikers' health deteriorates. An order goes out over the info-system: 'Everyone who doesn't mind or can stand the forcible feeding, go on refusing food. Everyone else – for instance, Andreas – stop at once. And damn it, that's an order!'

Outside, the headlines that summer are left to the June 2 Movement, who'd been given a boost by the return of Fritz Teufel (after doing two years in Hitler's old nick for attempted arson).

JUNE: The Berlin apartment/'bomb factory' of J2M member Angela Luther goes up in flames.

JULY 7: Gabi Kröcher-Tiedemann (J2M) is arrested in Bochum after a shootout.

JULY 27: J2M bank raid in West Berlin nets DM200,000.

AUGUST: Inge Viett (J2M) escapes from Berlin jail by sawing through her bars. Police attack workers attempting to occupy the Ford plant at Cologne; and a series of strikes virtually cripple the BRD.

OCTOBER 2: More J2M arrests in Berlin; and British Army practise 'repression of workers' strikes' in BRD.

NOVEMBER 13: Till Meyer (J2M) escapes from Castro-Rauxel prison.

DECEMBER 12: Gabi Kröcher-Tiedemann gets 8 years for attempted murder of a policeman.

JANUARY/FEBRUARY 1974: More large scale strikes; and police raids in Hamburg and Frankfurt, resulting in the re-arrest of Margrit Schiller, Ilse Stachowiak and Christa Eckes.

FEBRUARY 13: British Yacht Club bombing trial begins; Verena Becker, Wolfgang Knupe and Willi Rather stand accused. 50 demonstrators arrested and 25 police injured outside the court.

Back inside: the first sign of any relaxation of the 'isolation torture'. Gudrun Ensslin is moved to Ossendorf and put in the cell next to Ulrike Meinhof. They are even allowed to exercise together. But every silver lining comes with a cloud...

Stammheim prison, Stuttgart

APRIL: Ensslin and Meinhof become the first residents in the specially refitted high-security wing of Stuttgart's Stammheim prison. They still retain the right to exercise together plus 4 hours in the same cell each day, but their cells are now searched every day, a woman prison officer checks on them every hour and they're still banned from all communal activities (except visits from lawyers and family; and by this stage Ulrike Meinhof has broken off all contact with her children).

Baader, Meins and Raspe stay put for the time being in Schwalmstadt, Wittlich and Cologne respectively. With trials in the offing, preparations begin in earnest for the third hunger strike. Baader: 'I don't think we shall call the hunger strike off this time. That means some people will die...'

JUNE 4: Ulrich Schmucker, a former J2M member turned informant is assassinated; and SPK lawyer Eberhard Becker (husband of RAF lawyer Marielouise) is arrested.

AUGUST 27: Ulrike Meinhof is taken from Stammheim to Berlin Moabit, where she is to be tried along with Horst Mahler (again) and Hans-Jürgen Bäcker for their part in the Baader rescue. Ulrike says nothing until she's allowed to make a statement announcing the third hunger strike. This time their demands include: the right to strike, unsupervised visiting and an end to mail censorship. Horst Mahler, who Meinhof totally ignores at Moabit, doesn't take part in the hunger strike but he still gets 12 years for forming a criminal association (to run concurrently with the 14 he got for bank robbery). Ulrike gets 8 years and Bäcker gets acquitted.

SEPTEMBER 10: J2M members, posing as detectives, rob a Berlin arms store.

OCTOBER 2: Baader, Ensslin, Meinhof, Meins and Raspe are officially indicted on 5 murder charges. The trial is to begin in a year's time at Stammheim. (It's been delayed because Stuttgart

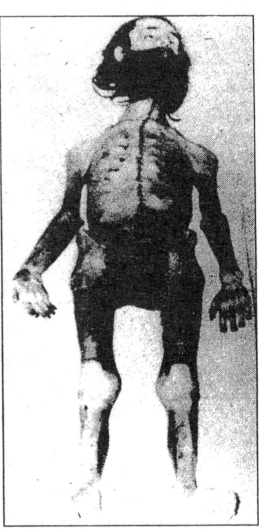

"I have kept this picture in my wallet to keep my hatred sharp" (Hans Joachim Klein). Holger Meins weighing just six stone eight pounds at the time of his death on 9 November 1974

was a host city for the 1974 World Cup). Baader and Raspe now join Ensslin and Meinhof in the Stammheim high-security wing.

Holger Meins stays put in Wittlich because his health has deteriorated so much. Prison doctors begin force feeding him and Ensslin. By the end of the month, virtually all the hunger strikers are being force fed. RAF lawyers, Klaus Croissant and Otto Schily charge the prison doctors with 'deliberate mistreatment and sadistic torture'. Force feeding is described by Holger Meins as a sort of aural enema; with the patient/ victim strapped down 'Clockwork Orange' style and his/her mouth levered open with a crowbar.

LATE OCTOBER: Manfred Grashof briefly gives up his hunger strike, but immediately resumes it when he receives a letter from Meins: 'Either a pig or a man, either survival at any price or a fight to the death, either problem or solution. There's nothing in between. Rather sad, having to write you something like this. Of course I don't know myself what it's like when you die or when they kill you... Ah well, so that was it. I was on the right side anyway... everybody dies anyway. Only question is how, and how one lived, and that issue's clear enough: fighting the pigs as a man for the liberation of mankind; a revolutionary in battle with all one's love for life, despising death.'

NOVEMBER 9: Holger Meins dies of starvation after presiding Judge Prinzing refuses to allow an outside doctor in to see him, and prison doctors ignore express instructions to transfer him to intensive care.

NOVEMBER 10: 'Avenge Holger Meins' demonstrations throughout Europe; several arson attacks on court buildings; and Günter von Drenkmann, President, of the Berlin Superior Court of Justice is shot and killed during a J2M kidnap attempt. RAF popularity is now at its zenith; imprisonment has only strengthened their political stature. From 1970 to '72 the police were after about 40 people; by 1974, this figure has leaped to 300 and the BKA has 10,000 names on its sympathisers' file.

JEAN-PAUL SARTRE GOES TO STAMMHEIM

1974/75: ACTION WINTER JOURNEY - THE PETER LORENZ KIDNAPPING AND THE STOCKHOLM EMBASSY SIEGE

NOVEMBER 26: 'Action Winter Journey' police raids throughout BRD; 80 apartments are raided, including RAF lawyers' offices from which trial documents are taken; 50 arrests are made but no significant ones.

Meanwhile, the hunger strike starts falling apart; Gerhard Müller, Margrit Schiller and Irene Goergens all come off. Ulrike Meinhof and Ingrid Schubert sympathise with Goergens, but Gudrun Ensslin condemns her as a sellout. Relations between Meinhof and Ensslin are at an all-time low. Baader remains remarkably neutral (and relatively un-misogynist), calling them both 'grotesque madwomen'.

DECEMBER: Gudrun Ensslin suggests, through the info-system, that somebody commits suicide every month until the isolation ends. Klaus Croissant has a more subtle (dare I say, existential) idea. He arranges for Jean-Paul Sartre to visit Stammheim, to interview Baader. The interview is never to be published – Sartre finds the RAF 'a danger to the Left' and Baader, like a true Punk Rocker, just finds Sartre 'OLD' – but the press presence assures plenty of publicity for the hunger strike.

DECEMBER 20: 'Baader-Meinhof Law' passed by the Bundestag, allowing the trial to continue in the absence of the defendants (if they have made themselves unfit to appear) and to bar lawyers suspected of 'supporting a criminal association'. Defence lawyer Ströbele is barred merely for describing himself as a socialist. Croissant, Groenewold and Lang are also barred, even though they've already been sacked by their clients.

FEBRUARY 2, 1975: Third RAF hunger strike called off after 140 days and the deaths of Holger Meins and Judge von Drenkmann. The RAF prisoners have now drawn out the battle lines for the next two years.

Jean-Paul Sartre and Klaus Croissant in front of Stammheim, December 1974

The RAF, inside and out, will now devote all its time and energy to freeing the prisoners.

Baader, Ensslin, Meinhof and Raspe are now allowed several hours together each day and almost daily visits from their lawyers. On the outside, Red Aid activists Angelika and Volker Speitel take over the running of the info-system from Klaus Croissant. After the death of Holger Meins, they go underground and join the remnants of the '4.2 Group' (Second generation RAF/SPK named after the date most of them got busted). From Stammheim the word comes out that this time they want to see less planning and more action.

FEBRUARY 27: Three days before the Berlin mayoral elections, Peter Lorenz, the leading Christian Democrat (CDU) candidate is kidnapped by J2M.

FEBRUARY 28: Along with a photo of Lorenz (with 'Prisoner of J2M' notice round his neck) the kidnappers demand: amnesty for those arrested at 'Avenge Holger' demos; the release of Horst Mahler, Verena Becker, Gabi Kröcher-Tiedemann, Ingrid Siepmann, Rolf Heissler and Rolf Pohle; to be accompanied to their destination by former Mayor Albertz (of Shah's visit fame); and while negotiations are in progress, a police cease fire – otherwise Lorenz will end up the same as von Drenkmann.

The demands are reasonable enough. Nobody convicted of murder is on the list; and there's no mention of the Stammheim Four, except a footnote: 'To our comrades in jail. We would like to get more of you out, but at our present strength we're not in a position to do it.' Horst Mahler is the only non-J2M member and he elects to stay put.

MARCH 2: Former Mayor/Pastor Albertz flies to Frankfurt, where he meets the J2M prisoners (and is bugged doing so, against his will) in a room under the airport complex. Then they all board a Lufthansa Boeing 707, each of the former prisoners is given $20,000 spending money and the take-off is shown live on TV.

MARCH 3: After being refused permission to land in Libya, the plane comes down at Aden in Yemen, and Pastor Albertz returns to Germany.

MARCH 4: Albertz appears on TV, giving the all clear line, 'a wonderful day like today', and Peter Lorenz walks free in the Berlin Volks Park with some small change to call his family. However, all the niceties stop there. An immediate nationwide search is launched for the J2M. Gerald Klopper and Ronald Fritsch are arrested merely for 'supporting the kidnapping'. And in return a J2M leaflet is circulated, detailing Lorenz's

Gabi Kröcher-Tiedemann prepares to take off for Aden with former Mayor Heinrich Albertz

corrupt career plus information extracted during his imprisonment in a Kreuzberg basement. (By the way, Lorenz receives 43% of the vote but loses the election which is held during his captivity.)

APRIL 25: As the finishing touches are given to the specially constructed courthouse at Stammheim, six former SPK members (Siegfried Hausner, Hanne-Elise Krabbe, Karl-Heinz Dellwo, Lutz Taufer, Bernhard-Maria Rössner and Ullrich Wessel) enter the West German Embassy in Stockholm.

Once inside, they produce guns, obtain the keys to the upper floors and take 11 embassy officials hostage. Swedish police subsequently occupy the ground floor and prepare to move up. Then one of the guerrillas calls down to the police, telling them to get out immediately or the German military attache will be shot. The police stay put. This is to be a lot messier affair than the Lorenz kidnapping.

At mid-day the RAF/SPK group call the German Press Agency and announce: "The Holger Meins Commando is holding members of the embassy staff in order to free prisoners in West Germany. If the police move in we shall blow the building up with 15 kilos of TNT." Then they repeat their demand to the Swedish police down below. There's still no response, so the German Military Attache, Baron von Mirbach is made to walk out onto the landing and shot. Two Swedish policemen (stripped to their underpants to show they're unarmed) drag the dying attache downstairs; and only then do the police retreat to the building next door.

After that the group contact the German Press Agency again and specify their demands. They want 26 prisoners freed in all, this time including Baader, Ensslin, Meinhof and Raspe. Chancellor Helmut Schmidt hears the news at Palais Schaumburg, and informs the assembled 'Crisis Staff' that he isn't prepared to deal this time. Then he

The German Embassy in Stockholm goes up in flames, April 1975

gives the go-ahead for an assault on the embassy by a special anti-terrorist squad. So that leaves the Swedish Minister of Justice nothing to negotiate with but safe conduct. The kidnappers aren't interested, and insist they'll shoot a hostage every hour until their demands are met.

10.20pm. The Economic Attache Hillegaart appears at a window, three shots are fired and the old man slumps forward. The Swedish police prepare to fire K62 stun gas into the upper floors, before storming the building. But before anybody has a chance to do anything the building is rocked by a series of explosions. The force of the blast throws three policemen to the ground and, along with window frames, guttering and office chairs, Ullrich Wessel is blown out into the embassy grounds. All the kidnappers and the hostages are badly burnt, but Wessel is the only one to die in the blast. However, despite particularly severe burns, Siegfried (no pun intended) Hausner is flown back to the BRD, where he dies of his injuries in Stammheim, evening the score. (It's later proved that the TNT was set off accidentally.)

MAY: Red lawyer Siegfried Haag, former partner of Klaus Croissant, and Elisabeth von Dyck arrested for smuggling arms out of Switzerland.

MAY 9: Karl-Heinz Roth (who warned Stefan Aust about Baader/Mahler), Werner Sauber and Roland Otto arrested after a shoot-out at a roadblock in Cologne. Sauber's wounds also prove fatal.

THE TRIAL

THE DEFINITION OF TERRORISM AND THE BAADER-MEINHOF GANG'S BILL GRUNDY

MAY 21: DAY 1 of the trial of Baader, Ensslin, Meinhof and Raspe begins at Stammheim. First of many objections to the court appointed defence lawyers raised by Ulrike Meinhof.

JUNE 5: DAY 2: Baader, still without a defence lawyer of his own choice, petitions for suspension of the trial until he's found one; and is allowed unsupervised conversations with lawyers. (Baader's claim that the prosecution is bugging cells used for lawyers' visits is scoffed at. But later the state has to admit that cells were bugged at the time of the Lorenz kidnapping and the Stockholm siege: 'two cases of justifiable emergency.')

JUNE 11: DAY 4: Baader allows Hans Heinz Heldmann to represent him. Heldmann immediately applies for a ten day adjournment to talk to his client and study the case files he hasn't yet been issued with. Then Otto Schily, defending Ensslin, asks for an adjournment on the grounds that the defendants are no longer fit to stand trial. When both applications are rejected, all the chosen defence lawyers walk out. Presiding Judge Prinzing then adjourns.

JUNE 15: DAY 5: Despite extensive cross-examination by Schily, Heldmann and Baader, prison doctor Henck maintains that the defendants are fit to stand to trial. After an adjournment there's more court-appointed defence lawyer baiting, ending in an uproar that the defendants have to create in order to leave the court.

JUNE 18: DAY 6: Baader reads out a statement on 'Fitness to stand trial': "The basic problem, on this point too, is the antagonism that calls for the state machine to make re-education, or brain washing, a legitimate project. That is, in order to subdue the subject the state machine must be able to constitute it. The cause at issue between the

repressive state machine and the captured revolutionary, however, is
that both know that in their irreconcilability, as in their relationship,
they express the maturity of the development wherein the contradiction
between productive forces and the circumstances of production becomes
antagonistic in the final crisis of capital, and thus the expression of the
trend whereby the legitimisation of the bourgeois state has fallen apart."

Judge Prinzing withdraws Baader's permission to speak. Then
Ulrike Meinhof applies for an examination by an independent doctor
because she is finding it difficult to follow the proceedings. Her
application is, needless to say, denied.
JUNE 23: Klaus Croissant and Hans-Christian Ströbele are arrested.
Croissant's Stuttgart office is raided and documents taken away,
causing a five day delay of the trial.
JULY 3: DAY 13: Jan-Carl Raspe makes the first of many challenges to
Prinzing and the court on grounds of bias.
AUGUST 5: DAY 23: Application after application has been made by the
defendants and their lawyers in order to raise the trial to a political level.
To get more directly to the point, Baader quotes an Interior Minister's
definition of terrorism: 'The basic rule of terrorism is to kill as many
people as possible. Numb horror is the state of mind terrorists obviously
wish to produce in more and more people throughout the world.'

Baader continues: "I would say that is the precise definition of
Israel's policy towards the Palestinian Liberation Movement, that is the
precise definition of the USA's policy in Vietnam, until its defeat... Numb
horror is, in fact, exactly the state of mind the Federal Prosecutor's
Office wants to produce in more and more people by having more and
more 'dead sections' built in prisons..."

Ulrike Meinhof warms to this 'state monopoly on terror' line:
"Terrorism is the destruction of utilities such as dykes, waterworks,
hospitals, power stations. All the targets at which the American bomb
attacks on North Vietnam were systematically aimed from 1965
onwards. Terrorism operates amidst the fear of the masses. The Urban
Guerrilla Movement, on the other hand, carries fear to the machinery of
the state."

The defendants are removed from court.

AUGUST 19: DAY 26: The defendants, having been expelled from the
courtroom for causing another disturbance, are recalled individually to
have their personal data examined. Judge Prinzing has been trying to
get to this initial stage of the trial (which comes before the reading of the
charges) since Day 1.

Jan-Carl Raspe is dragged into the courtroom by two prison guards.
Prinzing: "Please sit down."
Raspe: "I won't sit down."
Prinzing: "Then I must draw the following points to your attention. We

now intend to proceed to the examination of personal data."

Raspe: "That doesn't interest me."

Prinzing: "At this point you have an opportunity to give your own account of yourself. The consequence of your failing to do so will be that we must proceed with the trial."

Raspe: "All I have to tell you is that I've been dragged in here by force. In the circumstances I'm not giving an account of myself. I'm going down again now, and naturally you'll continue with this spectacle."

Prinzing: "It is your duty, as a defendant, to remain here."

Raspe: "If you won't expel me from court anyway, I'll climb out over this balustrade somehow."

Attempts to do so, but guards prevent him. Thereupon Prinzing decides to have Raspe removed. A few minutes later, Ulrike Meinhof is carried into the courtroom by four prison guards.

Prinzing: "Please sit down, Frau Meinhof."

Meinhof: "I've no intention of sitting down."

Prinzing: "You have no intention of sitting down. Would you at least make use of the microphone, so that we can hear what you have to say?"

Meinhof: "I don't want anything to do with this. I'm in no position to defend myself, and naturally I can't be defended either."

Prinzing: "Will you give an account of your personal details?"

Meinhof: "In these circumstances I will not give any account of my personal details."

Makes to leave the dock, but is stopped by the guards.

Meinhof: "I want to go."

Prinzing: "It is your duty, as a defendant, to remain here."

Meinhof: "I'm not letting anyone force me, you arsehole!"

Prinzing: "Frau Meinhof, I observe that you have just addressed me as 'arsehole', as 'you arsehole'."

Meinhof: "Perhaps you'll take note of that."

Prinzing, after consulting his colleagues: "The defendant is expelled from court for the rest of today's hearing for calling the presiding judge, 'You arsehole'."

Andreas Baader is brought in and refuses to sit down.

Baader: "Get on with it and expel me, will you?"

Prinzing: "Herr Baader, this is not a question of your own wishes."

Baader: "Then list all the disturbances, or do I have to call you names? I'm finding this very difficult. You want to force me to stay here?"

Prinzing: "It's not that I want to; I must."

Baader: "What are you waiting for, do you want to provoke abuse or what?"

Prinzing: "I don't want to provoke anything, I would far rather you refrained from abuse."

Baader: "I shall disrupt the trial, this manoeuvring of yours is a dirty trick."

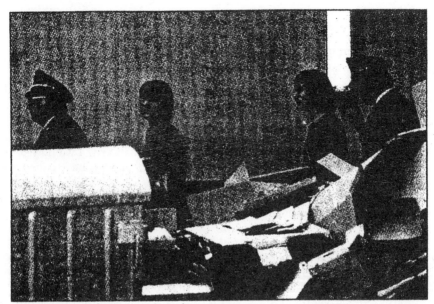

Meinhof and Ensslin being escorted into the courtroom

Prinzing: "There is no dirty trick involved. The rules of procedure oblige me to act as I do."

Baader: "So what do you want? Are you set on having physical violence here, or what?"

Prinzing: "I want you to sit down and take part in the hearing in an orderly manner."

Baader: "Hell, it's filthy manipulation, the way you're forcing me to spend five minutes insisting you expel me. I simply want to be out of here."

Prinzing: "It is not a question of your personal wishes. Your duty as a defendant is to remain here."

Baader: "Oh, alright, carry on with your ridiculous procedure. I shall create a disturbance."

Prinzing: "So far you are creating no disturbance."

Baader: "Well, let me tell you, Prinzing, you'd better expel me now or I'll find myself forced to abuse you."

Prinzing: "Herr Baader."

Baader: "Are you set on hearing it then? Alright, you can have it, you can have it all sorts of ways."

Prinzing: "I do not wish to hear it."

Baader: "Well, you can hear me tell you you're a Fascist arsehole."

Gudrun Ensslin is led into the courtroom and forced to stand in front of the dock.

Prinzing: "Ah, a 'Fascist arsehole'."
Baader: "Now will you expel me?"
Ensslin: "And me too, you old swine."
Baader: "I'll say it again, Prinzing, loud and clear; you're an old Fascist arsehole!"

Prinzing orders Baader's microphone to be switched off.

Ensslin: "We're not fit to stand trial, and owing to that we won't participate in this, you old swine."
Prinzing: "You have created a disturbance. I understood you to call me an old swine; did I hear that correctly or was I mistaken? I would like to have that ascertained; is it right? And you, Herr Baader, have called me a 'Fascist arsehole'."

Prinzing still asks Gudrun Ensslin if she will give an account of her personal details, the 'fucking rotter'.
Ensslin: "Old swine."

Then, finally, the personal data and charges are read in the defendants' absence: Andreas Baader, unemployed, Gudrun Ensslin, student, Ulrike Meinhof, journalist, and Jan-Carl Raspe, sociologist, are charged jointly with 4 murders, 54 attempted murders and with forming a criminal association.

Back on the outside: the June 2 Movement keeps itself busy. After the Lorenz kidnapping their most popular actions are the distribution of thousands of free U-bahn tickets, and two bank raids in West Berlin during which they give out chocolates to customers and staff. However, by September, J2M members Till Meyer, Ralf Reinders, Inge Viett, Julianne Plambeck, Fritz Teufel and Gabrielle Rollnick are all arrested and charged with the Lorenz kidnapping, the bank raids, and Reinders with the von Drenkmann assassination. Rainer Langhans and Dieter Kunzelmann settle down, and Bommi Baumann ends up in India with a guru, when he was meant to be getting arms. (Nowadays Dieter Kunzelmann is back in the public eye as a Green MP, and is responsible for the 'Alternative List' of the Berlin Chamber of Deputies.)

GIVE WAR A CHANCE

1975/76: THE OPEC RAID - CARLOS - THE DEATH OF ULRIKE MEINHOF - AND RAID ON ENTEBBE

DECEMBER 21: Vienna: Five gunmen shoot their way into a conference of 'The Organisation of Petroleum Exporting Countries' (OPEC). Three people are killed in the process: an Austrian policeman, an Iraqi bodyguard and a Libyan civil servant. The Austrian SAS immediately attempt to storm the conference room but are forced to retreat. The guerrillas holding 11 oil ministers and 60 others hostage, are a PFLP backed commando headed by Ilich Ramirez Sanchez, otherwise known as 'Carlos, the Jackal'.

Although the OPEC raid is to go down as Carlos' finest hour, the Venezuelan enigma is already renowned for, amongst other things: the attempted assassination of Edward Sieff, the British Zionist Chairman of Marks & Spencer; for orchestrating a Japanese Red Army assault on the French embassy in The Hague; and a rocket-launcher attack on an El Al jet at Orly airport. More than a match for the Austrian government, who soon capitulate, allowing the kidnappers safe passage,

Carlos the Jackal

with their hostages, to a destination of their own choice. The whole thing is basically a fund-raising, publicity exercise, forcing the OPEC countries to re-affirm support for the Palestinian cause.

The only snag is, during the Austrian SAS counter-attack, one of the guerrillas is seriously wounded. He is Hans-Joachim Klein, a member of the RAF/Red Aid offshoot 'Revolutionary Cells' (RZ), who acted as Jean-Paul Sartre's chauffeur when he visited Stammheim. While the negotiations are in progress, Klein is taken out of the OPEC building on a stretcher, and operated on in a nearby hospital. Even then, he is still in a critical condition. But Carlos and Klein himself insist that he be flown out with the others.

Hans-Joachim Klein stretchered out of the OPEC building

Algeria, who are particularly anxious to get their oil minister back in one piece, offers itself as the destination-country. And it all goes off smoothly and without further bloodshed. A little detour to Tripoli ensures that Iran and Saudi Arabia cough up contributions to the Palestinian cause in excess of $5 million. (Their ministers, Amouzegar and Sheik Yamani are top of the execution list.) All the remaining hostages are dropped off in Algiers, and Carlos follows Leila Khaled into the annals of terrorist folklore, never to be heard of again (outside of Frederick Forsyth/David Yallop fantasies).

JANUARY 1976: After court-appointed medical experts confirm that the Stammheim prisoners are not fit to stand trial for more than three hours a day, Judge Prinzing rules that the trial will be continued in their absence. The defendants officially admit to membership of an urban guerrilla group and claim 'political responsibility' for the various bomb attacks. After 8 months in court the actual trial now begins.

LATE JANUARY: Dierk Hoff, the metal sculptor, testifies for the prosecution.

FEBRUARY/MARCH: Communiques claiming responsibility for the bomb attacks are read out, and evidence is heard regarding the Heidelberg, Augsberg and Munich bombings. The defendants are seldom in court. Elsewhere, Gerhard Müller and Irmgard Möller get four and a half years, the Stockholm Embassy Siege trial begins in Düsseldorf, and Klaus Dorff and Jürgen Tauras (of the regional Ruhr group) are arrested in Cologne.

Boarding the getaway plane; Carlos is on the far left

APRIL: As evidence is heard about the controversial Springer building bombing, the conflict between Ulrike Meinhof and Gudrun Ensslin intensifies. Ensslin writes that she thinks Meinhof is 'trying to crack up' so she can get out of the RAF.

MAY 4: DAY 106: Ulrike Meinhof appears in court for the last time – not even staying to hear her defence counsel call for Richard Nixon, Willy Brandt and Helmut Schmidt to give evidence. The latest defence initiative is to show that the US government had violated international law with its military intervention in Laos/Cambodia/Nam; and because West German airbases were used, they could be considered as legitimate targets for international retribution.

MAY 9: Ulrike Meinhof is found hanging from the window grating in her cell. The official version: she tied a rope made from strips of towelling round her neck, climbed on a stool, attached the rope to the grating, and jumped. 'Suicide by strangulation. No extraneous factors.'

A second post-mortem, called by Ulrike's sister and defence counsel, agrees with the original findings. But later an 'International Investigatory Commission' finds evidence of possible rape: the initial chemical examination had got a positive reaction to a sperm test in the genital area. But further tests are all negative. There's also some doubt that the towelling rope could have been pushed through the grating without assistance of some kind. And most suspicious of all, there's no suicide

10 May 1976: a makeshift cross made from towels appears in a cell window at Stammheim as news leaks out of Ulrike Meinhof's death

note. Ulrike Meinhof had written about everything else she did, but not her 'final act of rebellion'.

MAY 11: DAY 109: After Ulrike's name has been struck from the court's agenda, Prinzing attempts to carry on as if nothing has happened. Raspe, Ensslin, Baader and the lawyers, Schily and Heldmann, all make applications for an adjournment and question the suicide verdict. Even the court-appointed defence lawyer Kunzel applies for an adjournment until after the funeral.

The Federal Prosecutor opposes all the applications, and all the defendants, defence lawyers and some of the spectators are either expelled or walk out in disgust. After the mid-day break, Jan-Carl Raspe makes a surprise reappearance and tells Prinzing: "I just wanted to say that your manner and function leave no way of relating to you except waiting in a corner with a gun."

Throughout Europe there are numerous demonstrations, most notably in Frankfurt and Berlin, and bombs go off at the West German consulate in Nice (claimed for the 'Ulrike Meinhof Commando'), the Kloekner and Thyssen buildings in Paris, and the USAF radio station in Frankfurt.

MAY 16: Thousands attend Ulrike Meinhof's funeral in Mariendorf, West Berlin. 26 of them are arrested.

JUNE 27: An Air France Airbus, full of Israeli tourists, is hi-jacked en-route from Tel Aviv to Paris. After a touch-down in Athens, the plane is redirected to Entebbe in Idi Amin's Uganda. In return for the hostages,

Ulrike Meinhof

the kidnappers demand the release of 40 prisoners held in Israel, five in Kenya, one in France, one in Italy and six in West Germany. Significantly the Germans do not include Baader and Ensslin, but Jan-Carl Raspe is named along with Ingrid Schubert and Werner Hoppe of the RAF, Fritz Teufel, Ralf Reinders and Inge Viett of J2M.

As immortalised in the various 'Raid on Entebbe' films, after as much stalling as possible the Israelis appear to be on the verge of conceding, then a crack commando unit is sent in. During the raid all the hi-jackers are killed, and all the hostages are freed and flown back to Israel. (Except the Brit Dora Bloch, who Idi Amin had for lunch.)

The chief of the German anti-terrorist squad (GSG 9), Ulrich Wegener, who went along as an advisor, gets shot in the hip while actually participating in the raid. ('Those GSG 9 boys just couldn't stay put.') But he isn't the only German involved in the affair: as Jillian Becker gleefully points out at the beginning of 'Hitler's Children', the hi-jackers include two RZ members, the founder and Carlos co-hort, Wilfried Böse and Brigitte Kuhlmann.

Becker sets the tone of her book by describing how the Israeli hostages are separated from the others. One of the hostages tells Böse that he's no better than his Nazi forebears: '...Böse replied that this was something quite different from Nazism... what they wanted was world Marxist revolution. To the hostages at Entebbe the difference was hard to see. The hostages did not die. As all the world knows, armed Israelis descended out of the sky on the day set for slaughter, gathered them up and carried them back through the air to safety in Israel. It was Böse and his comrades who were shot dead...'

EVERY CAPITALIST HAS A TERRORIST IN THE FAMILY

1976/77: THE FALL OF JUDGE PRINZING - THE ASSASSINATION OF FEDERAL PROSECUTOR BUBACK - THE VERDICT - KILLER IN THE HOME - AND STALIN'S ORGAN

Meanwhile, back in Stammheim...

JUNE 28: DAY 121: The defence calls two Americans who used to work for the CIA at the US military HQ in the IG Farben building in Frankfurt. (Incidentally, the IG Farben multinational was responsible for the 'Zyklon B' gas used in the concentration camps.) Their evidence would have been along the lines of the BRD being a party to war crimes committed by the US in Vietnam. Which would have led back to the RAF applying an 'international right to resist' with its actions. But their evidence is found inadmissible: 'The Vietnam war is not the subject of this trial.'

JULY 7: Inge Viett, Gabrielle Rollnick, Juliane Plambeck and Monika Berberich escape from Lehrterstr. maximum security prison in West Berlin. They simply overpower a guard and go over the wall.

JULY 8: DAY 124: Former RAF member, Gerhard Müller is called to give evidence for the prosecution. Müller has eventually given into police pressure to talk, in exchange for a reduced sentence.

JULY 21: Monika Berberich is recaptured in West Berlin, and Ralf Pohle is picked up in Athens. Pohle is eventually extradited after Chancellor Schmidt threatens Greece with heavy economic sanctions.

JULY 22: DAY 129: Brigitte Mohnhaupt, doing 4 years for membership of a criminal association, is called by the defence to refute the evidence of Müller (that the RAF has an authoritarian structure).

JULY 28: DAY 131: Klaus Jünschke, who has also been called to refute Müller's evidence, harangues Prinzing for a bit, then vaults the judges' bench and pulls Prinzing to the ground. (When Jünschke is sentenced the following year, his leap at Prinzing is cited as proof of his 'fanatical hatred' of the state. He consequently gets life for 'joint murder', committed during the Kaiserslautern bank raid, even though there isn't much evidence that he was even there.)

AUGUST 3: Baader and Raspe get extra charges against them after a punch-up on the 7th floor with two of the Stammheim guards.

AUGUST 4: DAY 134: Prinzing withdraws the prisoners' right to mingle in the 7th floor corridor.

OCTOBER: Rolf Pohle is re-arrested in Greece and extradited.

OCTOBER 14: DAY 253: Press reports that the RAF possess atomic devices discussed during the evidence of Federal Prosecutor Buback.

NOVEMBER 30: Siegfried Haag is rearrested along with Roland Mayer near Frankfurt. Haag had gone underground before the trial to help reconstruct the RAF. Police raids following his capture come up with photos taken inside Stammheim. When the trial resumes a week later the defence counsel are told to take off their shoes and open their trousers before entering court. Despite indignant objections the 'trouser edict' stands for the remainder of the trial.

DECEMBER 13: After a failed bank raid in Vienna, Sabine Schmitz and Waltraud Boock (of the Haag group) are arrested.

JANUARY 10, 1977: DAY 171: Otto Schily produces evidence that Judge Prinzing has passed on papers concerning the trial to Appeal Court Judge Mayer. Mayer, in turn, made the papers available to the press. Schily's evidence is a letter from Mayer to the editor of 'Die Welt', suggesting that he use the trial papers to discredit 'Der Spiegel'. Pretty damning stuff. Prinzing disallows the challenge, but the writing is on the wall.

Prinzing's final downfall comes when he calls the court-appointed defence lawyer, Künzel, who had once again supported a Schily challenge, and accuses him of letting the side down. Hans Heinz Heldmann uses this incident to issue the 85th challenge to the judge on grounds of bias. And that's Prinzing's lot, he's subsequently discharged and replaced by associate judge Foth.

EARLY FEBRUARY: More clashes on the 7th floor between the prisoners and guards.

FEBRUARY 9: Brigitte Mohnhaupt is released with remission and immediately goes back underground.

MARCH 15: DAY 184: After the bugging of nuclear scientist, Klaus Traube goes public, Otto Schily applies for the suspension of the trial until it can be proved that the defendants and their lawyers aren't being bugged also. Once again, Schily's application is found to be unfounded.

MARCH 17: DAY 185: Interior and Justice ministers admit to the press that during the Stockholm siege and after Haag's arrest, conversations were monitored. (But they don't admit that cells had been bugged since March '75, as is later revealed.) All the court-appointed lawyers back

Schily's motion to suspend the trial until the matter is cleared up. Judge Foth eventually adjourns.

MARCH 22: Top secret internal committee meeting of the Bundestag regarding the Stammheim bugging affair.

MARCH 29: DAY 187: Last appearance of the defendants. Baader makes an application for the two Social Democrat chancellors, Willy Brandt and Helmut Schmidt to be called, to face charges of persecuting the RAF since 1972 'according to a conception of anti-subversive warfare contrary to common law.' Jan-Carl Raspe applies for secret service men to be called to prove that they're bugging the 7th floor. And Gudrun Ensslin announces the 4th hunger strike. None of them appear in court again. (Neither does Manfred Künzel, the court-appointed defence lawyer, who walks out in disgust over the bugging affair, never to return.)

MARCH 31: Manfred Adomeit and Norbert Kröcher (Gabi's hubby) of the Haag group are arrested in Stockholm and accused of planning to kidnap Swedish cabinet minister, Anna-Greta Leijon.

APRIL 7: A Suzuki motorbike pulls up next to a Mercedes taking Federal Prosecutor Buback to the high court in Karlsruhe. The rider and pillion passenger of the Suzuki produce automatic weapons and shoot Buback, his driver and a colleague dead. Buback is responsible for all the RAF trials. The assassination is claimed by the 'Ulrike Meinhof Commando'.

APRIL 21: DAY 191: The penultimate day of the trial. The court-appointed lawyers sum up. The defendants send messages that they have nothing more to say.

APRIL 28: DAY 192: Presiding Judge Foth delivers the verdict. The defendants are found guilty of jointly committing 4 murders, in conjunction with 7 attempteds, and 27 other murders in conjunction with bomb attacks; Baader and Raspe have two more attempteds and Ensslin just the one; and they're all found guilty of forming a criminal association. Each gets life imprisonment.

APRIL 30: Stammheim governor Nusser agrees to bring a certain number of prisoners together. The 4th hunger strike is called off.

MAY/JUNE: Conversion of the 7th floor to accommodate the extra prisoners. For the first time RAF prisoners are able to associate with ordinary prisoners employed on the conversion job. (In theory this is the most likely time that anything – i.e. guns – could have been smuggled in.)

MAY 3: Günter Sonnenberg and Verena Becker (ex-J2M) are shot and captured during a shootout in Bonn. Two policemen are also wounded and Sonnenberg, who is wanted for the Buback killing, suffers irreparable brain damage.

MAY 4: Uwe Folkerts and Johannes Thimmes of the Haag group are arrested.

MAY 9: Hans-Joachim Klein renounces terrorism in 'Der Spiegel'.

MAY 13: Irene Goergens is released with remission; as is Dr. Wolfgang Huber of the SPK.

JUNE 2: Manfred Grashof and Klaus Jünschke get life. Wolfgang Grundmann gets four and a half, which he's already served so he's released.

LATE JUNE: Wolfgang Beer, Helmut Pohl and Werner Hoppe from Hamburg, join the three remaining Stammheim originals, Ingrid Schubert who's been there a year, and Irmgard Möller who arrived in January, making 8.

EARLY JULY: Klaus Croissant does a bunk to France.

JULY 20: Hanne-Elise Krabbe, Karl-Heinz Dellwo, Lutz Taufer and Bernhard-Maria Rössner each get twice-life for their part in the Stockholm Embassy Siege.

Christian Klar

JULY 30: Jürgen Ponto, head of the Dresdner Bank (Germany's second largest), unwittingly lets a RAF commando into his Oberursel home. One of them, Susanne Albrecht, is the daughter of an old friend of Ponto's. Once inside, her male companion, Christian Klar pulls out a gun and fires. There's a struggle and another girl, later identified as Brigitte Mohnhaupt, shoots Ponto five times. Apparently it was meant to have been a kidnap. Ponto dies in hospital.

AUGUST 5: Strange goings-on on the 7th floor; Irmgard Möller has permission to spend the night in Gudrun Ensslin's cell. However, contrary to all the rules, Andreas Baader is locked in with them as well. Nothing happens for an hour, then 8 prison guards charge down the corridor and escort Baader and Möller back to their cells.

AUGUST 6: Guards lock Baader and Ensslin's cells during association period. Relations between prisoners and guards tenser than usual.

AUGUST 8: More trouble over the locked doors; there's a bit of a scuffle between Raspe and one of the guards, then 30 prison guards storm the 7th floor. As a result of the ensuing turmoil, which appears to have been for no other purpose than for the guards to let off steam, Beer, Hoppe and Pohl are sent back to Hamburg and all the prisoners go on hunger strike again.

AUGUST 26: A couple visit the painter Theodor Sand and say they're interested in buying one of his paintings. The painter's house happens to be opposite the Federal Prosecutor's office in Karlsruhe. Around midday the couple make their move, easily overpowering Sand and his wife. Then a Renault van, with 'A. Krieg – Instant Customer Service' on its side, pulls up outside and a group of young people get out and carry metal objects up to Sand's apartment.

This is Peter Jürgen Boock's 'Stalin's Organ', a multiple rocket launcher which was to be trained on the Federal Prosecutor's office. However it takes Boock several hours to construct his creation and he later claims that he deliberately sabotaged it. Indeed the rocket launcher doesn't work, but the judge at Boock's trial doesn't believe his sabotage story and sentences him anyway.

The aborted Ponto kidnapping and rocket-launcher attack is the work of the second generation RAF, whose roll-call now reads: Brigitte Mohnhaupt, Sieglinde Hofmann, Elisabeth von Dyck, Christian Klar, Knut Folkerts, Sigrid Sternebeck, Angelika Speitel, Silke Maier-Witt, Willy Peter Stoll, Peter Jürgen Boock, Susanne Albrecht, Adelheid Schulz, Rolf Clemens Wagner and Stefan Wisniewski. So far they hadn't achieved much more than the intermediary SPK generation, but they were just warming up.

GERMAN AUTUMN PART 1

THE HANNS-MARTIN SCHLEYER KIDNAPPING: DEADLINES AND DELAYING TACTICS

SEPTEMBER 5: Despite clues aplenty and an armoured escort, employers leader and Daimler-Benz Chief Executive Hanns-Martin Schleyer is kidnapped in Cologne. His car and its police escort are forced to stop by a pram left out in the road. As soon as they do so, masked gunmen appear, shooting the three policemen and Schleyer's driver dead. Schleyer himself is bundled into a Volkswagen minibus and driven away. The BKA announces an immediate nationwide alert, and Justice Minister Vogel and Minister of State Wischnewski visit the scene. At Stammheim TV sets and radios are confiscated and Baader, Ensslin and Raspe are moved to new cells.

SEPTEMBER 6: The Volkswagen minibus is found along with a note demanding that all investigations be called off or Schleyer will be shot. BKA chief Herold flies to Bonn for an emergency meeting with Chancellor Schmidt. The two former Wehrmacht officers agree not to deal over the former SS man, Schleyer. Herold is confident that, with time, his computer will come up with a lead. So they don't tell the press about the letter in the minibus. That afternoon, another letter duly arrives at the house of a Protestant dean in Wiesbaden. It contains two photos – the famous one of Schleyer holding the 'Prisoner of the RAF' placard and one he had on him – and the kidnappers' (the 'Siegfried Hausner Commando') demands.

First they reiterate that if investigations don't stop immediately Schleyer will be shot; then in return for his release they demand that Andreas Baader, Gudrun Ensslin, Jan-Carl Raspe, Verena Becker, Werner Hoppe, Karl-Heinz Dellwo, Hanne-Elise Krabbe, Bernhard Rössner, Ingrid Schubert and Irmgard Möller be taken to Frankfurt airport the next day and flown to a country of their choice, accompanied by human rights activists Pastor Niemöller and Denis Payot. The letter concludes, optimistically: 'We assume that Schmidt, after he showed at the time of Stockholm how fast he comes to his decisions, will endeavour to clarify his relationship with this fat magnate of international economics just as quickly.'

Next it's announced on TV news that the kidnappers' letter arrived too late for the deadline to be met. Schmidt subsequently meets with the CDU opposition leader Kohl (today's Chancellor) and officially gets his approval of the hard line. After that an all-party 'Larger Crisis Staff' meeting is called. Schmidt makes his statement that there will be no capitulation to the kidnappers' demands; and as a first step the RAF prisoners are completely isolated from each other, their lawyers, everybody. (However, obviously tampered with radio equipment is returned to the prisoners, so that their short-wave broadcasts to each other can be monitored.)

SEPTEMBER 7: As a further stalling device, Herold asks the kidnappers, over the radio, to produce unmistakable proof that Schleyer is still alive. This is to take the form of taped responses to personal questions that only Schleyer can answer correctly, and is to be dragged out for six weeks. A video-tape of Schleyer's answers and fresh demands for TV coverage arrive at the homes of other priests. Once again, the BKA play for time, claiming that the tapes arrived too late for transmission and suggesting the use of an intermediary. The hunt for Schleyer is now in full swing, albeit discreetly and a strict news blackout is now imposed.

SEPTEMBER 8: The kidnappers' second letter is published (two days after it was received); the only concession so far.

SEPTEMBER 9: Another letter demanding a decision arrives at the French Press Agency in Bonn. Once again the letter isn't published. The kidnappers, obviously aware of what's going on, get Schleyer to write letters to old friends urging a quick decision. One to his son says if the delays go on he will be liquidated and someone else will be kidnapped.

SEPTEMBER 10: Denis Payot, the Swiss lawyer and human rights activist, agrees to be the intermediary. That night he is contacted and told that the next day one of the RAF prisoners is to appear on TV, to confirm that flight preparations are going ahead. However, there is a slight discrepancy in the Schleyer statement; he's given the wrong month of a meeting he attended. The BKA use this as an excuse to stall for more proof and start to ask for more specific details about the flight.

SEPTEMBER 12: A package is left in a Düsseldorf hotel containing more proof that Schleyer is still alive and a tape saying the ultimatum will be extended to midnight and only the RAF prisoners can say where they want to go. After more 'Smaller' and 'Larger Crisis Staff' meetings, a new communique is drawn up and conveyed to the kidnappers through Payot, saying preparations had begun and that the RAF prisoners will be asked where they want to go: The 4th ultimatum isn't met.

Hanns-Martin Schleyer: prisoner of the RAF

SEPTEMBER 13: Alfred Klaus of the BKA goes to Stammheim with flight questionnaires. Baader names Algeria, Vietnam, Libya, Yemen and Iraq as possible destinations, and says the government must ask the countries to accept them. Meanwhile Payot receives another message from the kidnappers, requesting that he cease his intermediary role because it's just being used as a delaying tactic. In response to their next midnight deadline the BKA make another token concession; they will begin negotiations with Algeria and Libya. The 5th ultimatum isn't met.

SEPTEMBER 14: Minister of State Wischnewski flies to Algeria and Libya. Another video-tape of Schleyer arrives at the French Press Agency in Bonn, and the kidnappers call Payot suggesting that the prisoners' departure be televised that night after closedown. Later TV detector vans scour an area of Cologne on a clairvoyant's advice. Herold's computer clearly isn't earning its keep.

SEPTEMBER 15-19: Minister of State Wischnewski flying about, acting busy. Questions and answers still going back and forth. The kidnappers tell the BKA: "All we have to say is that we are not going to spend another fortnight negotiating."

SEPTEMBER 20: New law passed at unprecedented speed, legalising the hitherto illegal total contact ban imposed on the RAF prisoners.

SEPTEMBER 22: Former SPK member Knut Folkerts arrested in Utrecht after a shoot-out which leaves one Dutch policeman dead and two more injured. A woman, identified as Brigitte Mohnhaupt manages to get away.

SEPTEMBER 24: More stalling by the BKA, who say they're expecting answers from four destination-countries shortly. The kidnappers call Payot again: "We are just wondering how long M. Payot is going to play this game. We are beginning to feel we have no time and no inclination to play it ourselves. End of message." Extensive wiretapping shows that most of the calls are coming from phone booths around Cologne train station, but a few are coming from Gare du Nord in Paris – Schleyer is fact being held in Brussels.

SEPTEMBER 25-27: Wischnewski in Vietnam. BKA tell the kidnappers that Libya and Yemen have refused to take the prisoners. The kidnappers tell Payot: "No more proof that Schleyer is alive will be given except with concrete indications of the exchange." Jan-Carl Raspe adds Angola, Mozambique, Guinea-Bissau and Ethiopia to the list.

SEPTEMBER 28: A Japan Airlines plane is hijacked by the Japanese Red Army, who demand the release of nine prisoners. The Japanese government concede to the hijackers' demands.

SEPTEMBER 30: BKA announce that Vietnam and Algeria have refused to accept the prisoners. Klaus Croissant arrested in Paris.

OCTOBER 1: Arndt Müller, the lawyer suspected of smuggling stuff into Stammheim, arrested in Stuttgart.

OCTOBER 2: Contact ban law comes into force, affecting 72 prisoners. BKA demand further proof of Schleyer's continued existence and refuse to bring the prisoners together. Volker Speitel is arrested when he returns from a protest tour of Denmark, and Klaus Croissant's Stuttgart offices searched again and sealed up.

OCTOBER 4: Police begin a search of a Cologne tower block, which they've had under surveillance for some time. A car with the same number plates as the one used in the kidnapping is parked in the underground garage. Police ascertain that Schleyer was brought there in the boot, and one of the apartments eventually turns out to be in Angelika Speitel's name. But by then it's long since been vacated.

OCTOBER 6: After Baader, Ensslin, Raspe and Möller issue identical appeals against the contact ban, prison doctor Henck reports that Raspe is suffering from severe depression and suicidal tendencies. Baader subsequently writes: 'Putting together all the measures adopted over the last six weeks, one can conclude that the administration is hoping to incite one or more of us to commit suicide, or at least to make suicide look plausible. I state here that none of us intend to kill ourselves. Supposing, again in a prison officer's words, we should be 'found dead', then we have been killed in the fine tradition of all the judicial and political measures taken during these proceedings.'

Palma de Mallorca: A young man books into the Saratoga Hotel, with an Iranian passport in the name of 'Ali Hyderi'. The following day he is joined by a girl with an Iranian passport in the name of 'Soraya Ansari'.

OCTOBER 8: A new picture of Schleyer, holding '31 days a prisoner' placard, arrives at Payot's office. In the accompanying handwritten letter, Schleyer pleads: 'The uncertainty is the worse thing to bear. In my first statement after the kidnapping, I said that the decision about my life was in the hands of the Federal Government and I thereby accepted that decision. But it was a decision I meant; I was not thinking of vegetating in constant uncertainty, in which state I have been for a month.'

Palma de Mallorca: A second apparently Iranian couple arrive and book in at the Costa del Azul hotel, near the Saratoga. Their Iranian passports are in the names of 'Riza Abbasi' and 'Shanaz Holoun'. 'Abbasi' books two first class tickets for Lufthansa Flight 181 to Frankfurt on October 13. At the same time 'Ali Hyderi' is booking two economy class tickets on the same flight. The Iranian couples are in fact another of Wadi Haddad's PFLP commandos: Hind Alameh, alias 'Shanaz Holoun', Nabil Harb, alias 'Riza Abbasi', Suhaila Sayeh, alias 'Soraya Ansari', and the leader, Zohair Youssif Akache, alias 'Ali Hyderi', who is already wanted for the assassination of the North Yemen prime minister in London.

At Stammheim, Baader, Ensslin, Raspe and Möller speak with the BKA man Klaus, and threaten to "take the decision out of Schmidt's hands by deciding for ourselves, in the way still open." Gudrun adds: "This is something that concerns the Government, because the Government is responsible for the facts which account for it; five years of torment and murder, the show trial, the constant electronic surveillance, torture by drugs and solitary confinement – the whole wretched ritual carried out to break our will and consciousness, and it is also responsible for the way this inhuman conception has been taken to extremes over the last six weeks; total social and acoustic isolation, and all the harassment and torments that are supposed to finish us off."

Then she repeats a promise that Baader had previously made; if they are exchanged and the Government doesn't try to extradite them back again, they have their assurance that they will not return to the BRD.

GERMAN AUTUMN PART 2

THE LUFTHANSA HIJACKING: ANNA-MARIA'S BIRTHDAY PARTY AND THE DEATH OF A PILOT

OCTOBER 13: 13.00 hours, German time: Lufthansa jet 'Landshut', a Boeing 737, flight no. LH 181, takes off from Palma de Mallorca for Frankfurt, with 86 passengers (including a party of beauty queens) and 5 crew on board. Just after take-off, two men rush into the cockpit and drag co-pilot Jürgen Vietor out into the gangway. Simultaneously two women stand up, holding hand grenades above their heads. The co-pilot, stewardesses and first class passengers are moved back to Economy, where they are re-seated with young men in the window seats. Over the intercom, the hijack leader, who remained in the cockpit, introduces himself as 'Captain Martyr Mahmud'.

14.38 hours: Air Traffic Control at Aix-en-Provence reports a deviation in the Lufthansa jet's flightpath. Two hours later it comes down at Rome's Fiumicino Airport, a thousand metres from the main terminal. Armoured vehicles surround the plane and 'Captain Mahmud' addresses the tower in English: "The group I represent demands the release of our comrades in German prisons. We are fighting against the imperialist governments of the world."

By this time, Interior Minister Maihofer is aware of the situation. From Bonn he gets Cossiga, his opposite number in Italy on the line and tells him: "Whatever happens the Lufthansa jet must not be allowed to fly on. Shoot out the tyres." But Cossiga isn't so sure. He consults Enrico Berlinguer, the leader of the Communist Party (at the time tolerated by Cossiga's Christian Democrat Party, not least because Berlinguer is related to Cossiga) and they agree that there will be no bloodbath on Italian soil. The plane is refuelled and takes off again at 17.42 hours. In Bonn, the 'Smaller Crisis Staff' has already decided to stick to its hardline.

19.55 hours: Another Lufthansa jet takes off from Frankfurt Airport, carrying Interior Ministry and BKA men. At a stopover at Cologne/Bonn Airport, they are joined by 30 highly trained and armed commandos of the special 'GSG 9' anti-terrorist unit, under the command of Ulrich Wegener, the Entebbe veteran.

20.30 hours: The hijacked jet lands at Larnaca. After refuelling again, it flies on.

23.13 hours: Shortly after the departure of the hijacked plane, the GSG 9 plane lands at Larnaca. It too refuels, then flies on towards the Persian Gulf.

OCTOBER 14: The Schleyer kidnappers contact Denis Payot in Geneva to announce that the passengers and crew of the Lufthansa 'Landshut' are under their control, and add the release of two Palestinians and a $15 million ransom to their demands. No more extensions of the deadline and no further contact. Any more delays will mean Schleyer's death. Schmidt, Maihofer, Wischnewski and Herold talk till 5 in the morning.

Meanwhile the hijacked plane lands in Bahrain and the GSG 9 men pursuing it are told to turn back. However their orders are soon altered; they are to await further instructions at Ankara in Turkey. From Bahrain, the hijacked plane flies on to Dubai, where 'Captain Mahmud' forces the pilot, Captain Jürgen Schumann to land despite the runway being blocked. At the last moment, the airport controller has the blockade removed on his own authority. The Dubai Minister of Defence arrives at the airport and asks the hijackers to release the women, children and sick. But Mahmud says there will be no compromise.

Things are getting very hot and bothered on the plane. Until, that is, Mahmud overhears the purser, Hannelore Piegler say, "What a day for a birthday," to the stewardess Anna-Maria Staringer. Mahmud immediately offers his own greetings and orders a birthday cake and champagne. The Dubai catering staff make a cake with 'Happy Birthday Anna-Maria' on it, and all the passengers are given a piece and some champagne.

While this is going on, the stewardesses write a message to Chancellor Schmidt – 'We put our lives in your hands, and ask you most fervently to save us' – on a picture postcard of the actual 'Landshut' aircraft. The other stewardess, Gaby Dillmann, asks Mahmud to sign it. Then he comes up with the idea of writing 'With Compliments of the S.A.W.I.O. (Struggle Against World Imperialism)' on the postcards and gives them out to the passengers as souvenirs.

But the party atmosphere soon changes when, during a baggage search, Mahmud discovers there are Israelis on board. After beating up one woman, he threatens to execute all the Israeli passengers the next day. Just before midnight, another Lufthansa jet lands at Dubai, unseen by the Landshut. On board are Wischnewski, a psychologist who has been advising the Government on the Schleyer kidnapping, and Gaby Dillmann's boyfriend, the co-pilot, Rüdiger von Lutzau.

Back in Bonn, Schleyer's son, Eberhard, agrees to meet the kidnappers' emissary to hand over the $15 million ransom, on condition that the other demands are met and no violent action is taken against the kidnappers while he's doing it.

OCTOBER 15: The German Press Agency announces that the Government are to meet the kidnappers' demand, that Eberhard Schleyer hand over the $15 million. Eberhard is flown to Frankfurt and taken to the Deutsche Bundesbank to collect the money (which is to be radioactively marked), but that's as far as he gets. The exchange is delayed because the 'Larger Crisis Staff' haven't reached a decision. Or so they tell Schleyer Junior. He isn't having any of it though, and gets his lawyers to appeal to the Constitutional Court for an interim injunction, forcing the Government to free the prisoners in order to save his father's life.

After being given the runaround some more by the Government, Eberhard finally gets to speak to the kidnappers, who aren't much better. They tell him to fly to Paris, from where he will take a long journey, destinations to be announced along the way, and at some point he will be approached by their emissary. The Government jump on this as too dangerous for Eberhard and too much of a risk that the money won't reach the right people. Kidnappers and Government finally agree to have the ransom given to the prisoners on their release. Horst Herold is very proud of this little scam of his, which saves the BRD $15 million.

Also, the Constitutional Court rejects Eberhard's appeal for their intervention: the Government has informed them of preparations for the GSG 9 unit to storm the plane, and basically they decide that Hanns-Martin Schleyer's life isn't as important as keeping the RAF prisoners locked up. While all this is going on, Alfred Klaus visits Stammheim again with another questionnaire: this time asking for the prisoners' approval of the hijackers' suggestion of Somalia as a possible destination. Baader says he'd prefer Vietnam, who he knows are prepared to take them, but if the PFLP commando really did say Somalia, it's okay with him. The same goes for the others.

OCTOBER 16: Ulrich Wegener, the GSG 9 commander, and Major Alistair Morrison and Sergeant Barrie Davis of the SAS, start training Bedouin troops. The Dubai Minister of Defence won't allow the GSG 9 unit to perform on his territory. However Mahmud starts threatening to shoot the pilot if the aircraft isn't refuelled -- During the night the power had failed on the plane and the air conditioning cut out. Captain Schumann eventually persuaded Mahmud to allow a generator to be brought out to the plane. But Mahmud realised the men who brought it out were German.

In the morning, he forces Schumann to kneel in the gangway and points his gun at his head, accusing him of sending messages out. The Dubai Defence Minister had praised the captain over the radio for passing out coded information: four unlit cigarettes in the rubbish, indicating the number of hijackers. And Mahmud was listening.

After making Schumann march up and down the gangway, Mahmud repeats his threat, adding that after the pilot he'll shoot a passenger every five minutes. The plane is refuelled pretty sharpish. More threats and the generator is disconnected. And at 15.19 hours, local time, the Lufthansa jet takes off for Aden.

During the flight the hostages are tied up and plastic explosives fixed to the cabin wall. Then, despite being refused permission to land again, co-pilot Vietor manages to bring the plane down on a track next to Aden airport. As soon as it comes to a halt the plane is surrounded by

Zohair Youssif Akache — alias Captain Martyr Mahmud — posed for this poster in a Soho gift-shop as a joke

hundreds of Yemeni troops. Schumann and Mahmud speak to them over a loudhailer but don't get any response. Finally Mahmud allows Schumann out to check the body-work. An hour passes. Mahmud becomes very agitated and says: "If the pilot doesn't come back, I'm blowing the plane up. If he does come back, I'll execute him."

Schumann does come back and, true to his word, Mahmud orders the pilot to his knees and says: "This is a revolutionary tribunal. You put everyone here in danger of being blown up. You've betrayed me once already. I'm not forgiving you a second time. Are you guilty or not guilty?" Schumann tries to explain, but Mahmud strikes him in the face, "Guilty or not guilty?" Schumann tries again, but Mahmud hits him even harder then shoots him in the head.

16.21 hours, German time: Minister of State Wischnewski's plane takes off from Dubai. South Yememi airspace is closed to it also, so it flies on to Saudi Arabia and lands at Jedda.

The body of Captain Jürgen Schumann dumped onto the runway at Mogadishu

HEROES

OCTOBER 17/18, 1977: POLITICIANS, PRIESTS AND PSYCHOLOGISTS - FIRE MAGIC AT MOGADISHU - THE JOB'S DONE AND THE NIGHT OF STAMMHEIM

OCTOBER 17: 2.02 hours, German time: The refuelled Lufthansa plane takes off from Aden, with the body of Captain Jürgen Schumann propped up in a cupboard.

4.34 hours: Co-pilot Jürgen Vietor brings the plane down in the Somali capital, Mogadishu.

7.09 hours: Wischnewski's Lufthansa jet takes off from Jedda, to join the hijacked plane at Mogadishu 4 hours later. Mahmud sees it arrive and radios the tower: "Tell the German representative there's nothing for us to talk about. I don't want to speak to him unless he can tell me the prisoners in Germany have been released." Then he adds: "We won't be needing anymore to eat. Our deadline runs out in 3 hours, and after that everyone will either be dead or free." The body of Captain Schumann is dropped out of the plane via the emergency chute.

Meanwhile at Stammheim, an unexpected critic of the hijacking is making a statement. Andreas Baader has finally got to speak to a politician, albeit an Under-Secretary Hegelau, representing Under-Minister Schüler, who doesn't know anything about the case. Baader begins: "It's really too late for this conversation. The chance of exerting any influence has been lost now." Then, with nothing to gain from it, he says the original RAF never condoned operations involving innocent civilians, but the Government had to realise that the new generations would be more brutalised and consequently more brutal.

"We don't know Schleyer's kidnappers and other people the police are after personally. If the BKA's saying these operations were masterminded from prison, that can't be so except in the ideological area. The armed combat has internationalised itself. It could be the

Japanese or the Palestinians who are going to decide the course of events now."

In an almost confessional manner, Baader goes on to say that he still feels their reaction to the Vietnam war was a justified one, but he admits they made mistakes and played into the state's hands. He concludes by saying that the prisoners would have to die one way or another.

Gudrun Ensslin actually gets a Catholic priest for her confession. (And a Protestant one for good measure.) The priests had been sniffing around do-gooding, since the total contact ban pricked a conscience somewhere. Contrary to Baader for once, Gudrun gives the priests the 'By Any Means Necessary' line; but the main reason she calls them is an 'If anything happens to me' request. She tells the priests to make sure that three sheets of paper, in a file marked 'Lawyer' in her cell, make it to the Chancellor in the event of her death. The priests listen politely, dutifully tell the governor and nothing more is ever heard of the three sheets of paper.

At Mogadishu, the hijackers' ultimatum is extended to 15.00 hours, German time. Wischnewski is in conference with the Somali government, desperately seeking their permission to send the GSG 9 unit in. In the meantime, the Somali Chief of Police is talking to the hijackers, telling them that the German government won't accept their demands but if they release the hostages, the Somali government will promise them asylum. Mahmud comes to the mike again: "That doesn't alter anything. We shall blow the plane up as soon as the deadline runs out, that is in exactly 34 minutes...If you happen to be in the tower then, you'll see the plane explode into a thousand pieces..."

Then he allows the stewardess, Gaby Dillmann, to speak to the German envoy. Unbeknown to her, her boyfriend, the co-pilot Rüdiger von Lutzau, is transcribing the radio communication in the other plane. She says: "We know it's the end now. We know we shall have to die. It will be very hard for us, but we'll die as bravely as we can. We're all too young to die, even the old are too young to die. We just hope it will be quick and we don't feel too much pain. But perhaps it's better to die than to live in a world where something like this is possible. Where it's more important to keep 9 people in prison than to save 91 lives. Please tell my family it wasn't too bad. And please tell my boyfriend – his name's Rüdiger von Lutzau – that I loved him very much. I didn't know there were any such people as the members of the German government who are partly responsible for our death. I hope they can live with this on their consciences."

Plastic explosive had been fixed to the cabin walls again and all the passengers tied up and doused with alcohol. Next, the Somali Minister of Information tries for another 24 hours. After a curt "There's no alternative to blowing up the plane in exactly 23 minutes from now", he comes down dramatically to half-an-hour so that the near vicinity can be evacuated. Mahmud says he'll consider it. Then the German charge d'affaires in Mogadishu has a go. "I am listening, representative of fascist imperialist West Germany," Mahmud jeers, "Go on, read out your message."

The charge d'affaires tries the 'very important news coming shortly' approach, 'once we've overcome a technical hitch'; the Somali President himself was speaking with the Chancellor of the BRD on their behalf. Mahmud begrudgingly gives them the half-hour to clear the vicinity. The Somalis take their time and 12 minutes after the new deadline expires, the German charge d'affaires comes back on the line. This time he says the German government has capitulated after all and the RAF prisoners will be along shortly. Well, in a day...

"You dare to ask me to extend the deadline until morning – is that it, representative of the West German fascist regime?" replies Mahmud. "In principle, yes." (The psychologist, Wolfgang Salewski is advising the charge d'affaires on everything he says – but it could so easily have been Eric Idle.) Then the charge d'affaires asks if he can go off to check how far it is from Germany to Mogadishu. Mahmud replies: "Okay, four minutes to go before the deadline runs out. If you're trying to trick us or play games with us... I'd rather play with explosive..." But he eventually relents and agrees to extend the deadline to 3.30 hours, local time (1.30 hours, German time). The hostages are untied again.

The GSG 9 unit, which had flown back to Cologne/Bonn the previous day, is reactivated along with another two units. A Lufthansa Boeing 707 carrying all three units takes off, initially destination unknown. It refuels at Crete and when Chancellor Schmidt gets permission from the Somali President to send them in, it is circling over Djibouti.

19.30 hours, local (17.30 German): Under cover of darkness, the GSG 9 plane lands at Mogadishu, 2,000 metres from the hijacked plane. No one on the 'Landshut' notices its arrival. They are busy deciding which hostages to exchange for which RAF prisoners.

OCTOBER 18: The GSG 9 squads take 2 hours to unload their equipment. In the meantime Ulrich Wegener crawls up to the Landshut, to check out the terrain; and the charge d'affaires, obviously prompted by the psychologist, keeps Mahmud occupied.

Lying again that the prisoners had left Germany at 19.20 hours (German), he almost pushes his luck too far, saying they won't arrive in Somalia until 4.08 (German) – after the new deadline. But Mahmud accepts it. Then the charge d'affaires strings him along some more, letting Mahmud give him instructions for how the exchange should take place:

"No one to approach the Lufthansa aircraft, commanded by the Halimeh unit without previous permission."

"Understood."

The GSG 9 shock troops are by now approaching the Lufthansa aircraft (albeit crawling along the ground with blackened faces), with previous permission alright, but not from Captain Mahmud...

"We'll make further arrangements with the comrades coming from Turkey."

"Would you repeat that?"

Mahmud obliges. It's his last full sentence.

"Understood."

"If they come..."

At this point the SAS stun-grenades go off outside the cockpit, incapacitating Mahmud. It is 0.05 hours, German time. Before the dazzling effect of the grenades wears off (6 seconds), Ulrich Wegener has the front door open. Simultaneously three more GSG 9 squads come in through the emergency exits and rear door.

Blanks are fired into the air to make the hostages get down. Then they switch to live ammunition. One of the girl hijackers dies instantly,

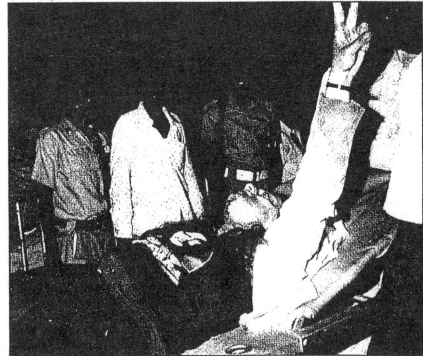

The sole surviving hijacker, in a Che Guevara T-shirt, gives the victory sign

the other dives into the toilet and shuts the door, which disintegrates in a hail of bullets. Miraculously she is the only hijacker to survive.

Mahmud is shot dead in the cockpit. The other man, Hind Alameh, gets a shot in before he gets his. The plastic explosive goes off to add to the mayhem, but does little damage – compared with what the GSG 9 men are doing anyway – the stewardess, Gaby Dillmann gets a slight leg injury from it. And that was it.

0.12 hours, German time: All the passengers safely off the plane via the emergency chutes, Minister of State Wischnewski reports back to Bonn: "The Job's done."

0.38 hours: Stammheim: News of the hostages release comes over the radio in the 7th floor guards' room. The guard on duty, ironically named Springer, checks on the prisoners. His night duty report reads: '23.00 hours. Baader and Raspe given medicaments, otherwise no incidents.'

THE OFFICIAL VERSION: Springer and his colleagues are the last people to see any of the prisoners alive, when they tuck Baader and Raspe in at 11.00 pm. Then Jan-Carl Raspe hears the news from Mogadishu on a small transistor radio he has concealed in his cell. He tells the others over the tampered with intercom, and they agree on a suicide pact.

In Cell 719 Baader has a 7.65 calibre FEG pistol, which had been concealed in Cell 715 during the alterations. (When he returned to his original cell, he brought it with him and hid it in his record player.) To give the impression of a struggle, he fires a few shots around. Then he puts the empty cartridges by his bed, reloads, puts the barrel of the gun to the nape of his neck and blows a hole through his forehead.

In Cell 716 Jan-Carl Raspe has a 9 mm Heckler and Koch pistol behind the skirting board. He puts the barrel of the gun to his temple, 'Deer Hunter' style, and fires.

In Cell 720 Gudrun Ensslin ties an electrical chord to the grating above her window and, like Ulrike Meinhof, stands on a chair, ties the other end of the chord round her neck and kicks the chair away.

In Cell 725 Irmgard Möller pulls up her sweater and stabs herself 4 times in the chest with a table knife.

THE FACTS: Irmgard Möller survives, and her version of the night's events is somewhat different to the official one. She reads until 4. Then before going to sleep, calls out to Raspe, who responds normally. She doesn't undress because she thinks they're about to be released. At 5 she hears thudding and squealing sounds, and the last thing she remembers, before she comes to on a stretcher, is "a loud rushing noise" in her head. She denies there was ever any suicide pact.

There are also 5 independent witnesses in the cells below. None of them hear any shooting, although Baader is heard flushing his toilet at 2.

Baader, Ensslin and
Raspe: suicide at
Stammheim?

The exact time of Baader and Ensslin's death cannot be ascertained because it takes over 12 hours to fly in independent foreign experts. Jan-Carl Raspe dies in hospital. At least he gets out of Stammheim alive.

Discrepancies in the official enquiry are manifold. Scientific evidence that the bullet which killed Baader was fired from 30 to 40 cm away is covered up. The mysterious sand on Baader's shoes is never properly accounted for. (There's even a theory that Baader was flown to Mogadishu to trick the hijackers, shot there and flown back.) Irmgard Möller's sweater, which could have proved it wasn't murder, is inexplicably cut to shreds. Nobody asks if the emergency monitoring methods (ie. bugging), used at the time of Stockholm/Lorenz, were in use. And nobody is allowed to ask anything about the Crisis Staff meetings, and they still aren't.

OCTOBER 19: The French newspaper, 'Liberation', receives the final communique from the Schleyer kidnappers:

> 'After 43 days of captivity we have put an end to the corrupt and
> miserable existence of Hanns-Martin Schleyer. Herr Schmidt, who from the
> start has been reckoning with Schleyer's death in his power calculations,
> can find him in a green Audi 100 with Bad Homburg number plates in the
> rue Charles Peguy in Mulhouse. His death in no way measures up to our
> grief and anger over the slaughter at Mogadishu and Stammheim. We
> will not forget the blood spilled by Chancellor Schmidt and the imperialists
> who support him! The fight has only just begun!'

Schleyer's body is found in the boot of the Audi near the French/German border. He has been shot three times in the head.

In Rome four policemen are wounded and 25 demonstrators arrested, when a march on the West German embassy turns into a pitched street battle. There are also at least 20 bomb attacks on German businesses throughout Italy.

In France two German car warehouses and many a Mercedes gets torched. A Mercedes-Benz garage in Limoges is burnt down with the word 'Vengeance' written on the one wall left standing. A German paper company in Toulouse is razed to the ground and a German owned factory in Versailles bombed. 'Andreas Baader Group of the Armed Faction Movement' claim responsibility. (Not quite as catchy as 'Action Directe' who are on their way.)

In Greece two policemen are wounded during a shootout with four guerrillas attempting to bomb a German electronics factory near Athens.
OCTOBER 21: The biggest manhunt yet is launched in Germany and France for the Schleyer kidnappers (believed to be: Susanne Albrecht, Christian Klar, Jorg Lang, Willy Peter Stoll, Elisabeth von Dyck, Silke Maier Witt, Adelheid Schulz, Sigrid Sternebeck, Angelika Speitel,

Friederike Krabbe, Juliane Plambeck, Inge Viett, Brigitte Mohnhaupt, Rolf Heissler, Rolf Clemens Wagner and Christoph Michael Wackernagel). Every possible form of media throughout Europe is used to broadcast the suspects' descriptions.

OCTOBER 27: Andreas Baader, Gudrun Ensslin and Jan-Carl Raspe are buried in a communal grave at Stuttgart's Waldfriedhof cemetery. A thousand policemen with sub-machine guns are there to see them off, and also to catalogue and search the mourners.

A banner reading 'GUDRUN, ANDREAS AND JAN WERE TORTURED AND MURDERED AT STAMMHEIM. THE FIGHT GOES ON.' is held up by demonstrators wearing PLO kaffiyehs.

The funeral: 'Gudrun, Andreas and Jan were tortured and murdered at Stammheim'

'"We must neither govern nor be governed," writes Marcel Havrenne so neatly. For those who add an appropriate violence to his humour, there is no longer any salvation or damnation, no place in the universal order, neither with Satan, the great recuperator of the faithful, nor in any form of myth, since they are living proof of the uselessness of all that. They were born for a life as yet to be invented, it was on this hope that they finally came to grief.'

RAOUL VANEIGEM, *BASIC BANALITIES*, 1962

'Yet that the students, being young, should be emotional does not seem to require special explanation. The emotion was no doubt sincere, but the causes of it may not have been the ones they flattered themselves by laying claim to. They got a regular stirring up from the media – pity and indignation roused on behalf of story characters, existant or not, learning about wars, exploitations, oppressions in the same way as they learnt about the fate of fictional victims, they felt strongly not because they were a generation of visionaries but because they were a generation of televisionaries.'

JILLIAN BECKER, *HITLER'S CHILDREN*, 1977

The Mail on Sunday, November 8, 1987

Femail ON SUNDAY

PAGE 23

Taming of Astrid the terrorist

COTSWOLD WOOLLENS

NATIONAL GARDEN GIFT TOKENS

THE SELF-ASSURED woman sitting in a top Hamburg restaurant sent back the wine — it wasn't the right vintage — then turned her attention to the subject of her brother's children.

She thinks they are not being brought up strictly enough, with proper respect for other people's property.

Yet ten years ago this woman was involved in arson attacks on Frankfurt department stores, drove the getaway car for a terrorist gang, and was imprisoned for shooting two policemen.

Astrid Proll, 40, was a founder member of the Baader Meinhof terror gang, the group who invented terrorism as a modern political weapon.

The gang called itself the Red Army Faction. Together they terrorised Germany, then spread their influence to Italy, Ireland, Israel and South America.

By 1970 they were directly responsible for 31 murders in Germany. Their aims were simply to rid West Germany of the American military presence, and to unseat the overthrow of capitalism.

All well-educated middle-class children, they moved easily from student radicalism to political assassination.

Armed struggle

Once one of the most wanted terrorists in Europe, Astrid is now the only survivor of the original Baader Meinhof. She

unleashed a spiral of hatred and death. But it was going to England that made me realise how much less repressive than mine.

'I'd never met poor people until I lived in the East End. The boys I worked with made my help, and as I began to register ...

THEN: Astrid and Andreas Baader

NOW: Survivor Astrid Proll
Picture LYNN MILTON

Jane Kelly meets a gun girl who wants to live in

THINKING OF SPONSORING A CHILD

SEXY SECRETS OF TERROR GIRL

THE secret life of terror girl Astrid Proll began to emerge yesterday.

Friends told of her lesbian loves, her delight at being a mechanic, and her strange obsession for consumer goods.

But the central and nagging question remained unanswered: How did Astrid Proll, one of the world's most wanted terrorists, get away with it all for so long?

She has been sought by West German police since 1974 when she fled her trial as a member of the notorious Baader-Meinhof gang.

Once in Britain, Astrid posed as Anna Puttick and said she had left Germany to escape a violent husband. She

ASTRID PROLL
Obsessed by gadgets

Sunday Mirror Reporter

trained as a car mechanic at a Government-run skill centre in Poplar, East London.

Then she got a £4,000-a-year job at a garage in Swiss Cottage, North London, as an instructor to unemployed youths.

Astrid, 31, lived in London's squatting community — never staying for long in the same house and always moving on if police threatened to take action against a squat.

For a time she shared a squat in Kilburn with one of her fellow instructors Johnny Mock-

He said: "Anna never made a secret of being a lesbian.

"At a party she took a fancy to a man sometimes. Most of her romances were short lived."

Another girl who lived in a squat with Astrid told how the German collected washing machines and fridges. She

was almost obsessed by gadgets," said the girl.

"She carried around loads of worldly goods."

The girl said that Astrid never talked of politics but was an ardent supporter of Women's Lib movement.

Astrid is now awaiting extradition. Scotland Yard yesterday took the first step by obtaining a special warrant.

CAMP DAVID 'COLLAPSE'

ONLY a miracle can save the Camp David summit meeting between the leaders of Israel and Egypt, Egyptian newspapers said yesterday. Israel was not making any real concessions and warned of a fifth Middle East war. Meanwhile, 60,000 Israeli troops moved close to the Lebanese border.

POSTSCRIPT: EUROTERRORISM

1977-1993: McDONALDS IMPERIALISM AND THE MILITARY INDUSTRIAL COMPLEX - BRIGATE ROSSE - ACTION DIRECTE - CCC - RAF: THE THIRD GENERATION

Stammheim/Mogadishu knocks the wind out of the RAF's sails somewhat. The Second Generation regroups in Aden, but by the early 80s most of them are rounded up or liquidated, one way or the other:

NOVEMBER 13, 1977: Ingrid Schubert, like Meinhof and Ensslin before her, is found hanging in her cell at Stadelheim-Munich. The news is greeted by more demonstrations and guerrilla actions throughout Europe.

DECEMBER: Klaus Croissant is extradited from France and jailed for aiding and abetting the RAF.

DECEMBER 20: Gabi Kröcher-Tiedemann (J2M) is arrested along with Christian Möller, after a shoot-out at the Swiss/French border; and ends up getting 15 years.

APRIL 11, 1978: The beginning of the 'Lorenz/Drenkmann' trial at Moabit. J2M founders Ralf Reinders, Ronald Fritzch, Gerald Klopper, Fritz Teufel, Till Meyer and Andreas Vogel, have their own 'Stammheim' style show-trial and receive equally long sentences.

MAY 27: During the proceedings Till Meyer manages to escape again. This time he is sprung by two female J2M members who enter Moabit with lawyers' ID, then produce guns and demand the release of Meyer and Andreas Vogel. A guard grabs a gun and locks Vogel in a cell, but the two women and Meyer get away after shooting another guard in the leg.

MAY 31: A court-appointed J2M defence lawyer is also shot in the leg and another has a narrow escape when a bomb planted in his car fails to go off. RZ (Revolutionary Cells) claim responsibility.

JUNE 21: Till Meyer is recaptured in Bulgaria, along with Gabrielle

JUNE 2nd
MOVEMENT

Rollnick, Gudrun Strumer (no relation as far as I know) and Angelika Godel.

JUNE 30: Brigitte Mohnhaupt, Sieglinde Hofmann. Peter-Jürgen Boock and Rolf Wagner arrested in Yugoslavia, but later freed and flown to an undisclosed country of their choice.

JULY 14: After the sentencing of Gabi Kröcher-Tiedemann and Christian Möller a bomb explodes at the Bern Court house, next to the prison where they're being held.

AUGUST 20: Astrid Proll is finally arrested in London and duly extradited.

SEPTEMBER 7: Willy Peter Stoll is gunned down in a Düsseldorf restaurant.

SEPTEMBER 25: Angelika Speitel and Michail Knoll are captured after a gun battle near Dortmund, which leaves one policeman dead.

OCTOBER: RAF lawyer Kurt Groenewold is found guilty of 'supporting a criminal organisation' and gets 2 years, although he's already done 3.

EARLY 1979: Elisabeth von Dyck is shot dead by police in Nuremberg.

JUNE 29: Unsuccesful attempt by RAF (Rolf Clemens Wagner/Werner Lotze) to blow up NATO chief, General Al Haig, as he drives to SHAPE (Supreme HQ Allied Powers in Europe) in Belgium.

1980: Juliane Plambeck and Wolfgang Beer are killed in a car crash. Adelheid Schulz, the driver survives.

MAY: After a raid on a RAF/J2M safe-house in Paris, Sieglinde Hofmann is arrested again along with Ingrid Barabass, who is suspected of kidnapping Austrian textile millionaire Walter Palmers.

AUGUST 31, 1981: RAF blow up propane gas canisters on the USAF base at Ramstein seriously injuring 17 people.

SEPTEMBER 15: Following a big demo in Berlin against the visit of Al Haig (now US Secretary of State), RAF narrowly fail to assassinate General Frederick Kroesen (Commander of US Forces in Europe) in an RPG 7 grenade-launcher attack.

OCTOBER 1982: After further attacks on US military bases, a RAF arms cache is discovered in woods near Frankfurt. The site is staked out by GSG 9 men and in due course Brigitte Mohnhaupt and Adelheid Schulz walk into the trap. Coded notes found with the cache lead to 14 other arms dumps and Christian Klar. These arrests are almost as big a blow to the RAF as those of Baader, Ensslin and Meinhof. But the group is never entirely wiped out. Inge Viett, Susanne Albrecht and Sigrid Sternebeck remain at large throughout the 80s, and in 1982 alone there are 600 bomb attacks in the BRD.

After the Klar/Mohnhaupt/Schulz bust (and subsequent trial for the Schleyer slaying), the RAF restructures itself along the lines of the later SPK: a hardcore of 20 or so organise and carry out the more important actions; then there's a 'Fighting Unit' buffer of about 200 people who provide safe-houses, cars and suchlike; and for further support they can call on several thousand 'Sympathisers' from the squatting and anti-nuclear movement. The RAF also continue to co-exist with RZ, who operate in cells of no more than ten people, and avoid loss of life in their attacks on nuclear power stations, computer companies and the like, as do 'Rote Zora', the all-women group.

But as Andreas Baader predicted in his final statement, after the deaths of the RAF founders things internationalised. Most notably (and debatably) in Italy, where the 'Red Brigades' came closest to bringing down their admittedly never too stable state. Founded by Renato Curcio

Aldo Moro

in 1970, 'Brigate Rosse' could claim closer links to your actual workers than any other European guerrilla group. Curcio himself is captured in 1974, sprung in 1975 and recaptured in 1976 before BR gets serious.

JUNE 1976: The Genoa Prosecutor-General Francesco Coco and his two bodyguards become the first BR assassination victims.

1977: More BR attacks on judges, industrialists and journalists, leading up to their big attack at 'the heart of the state'...

MARCH 16, 1978: BR activities culminate in the kidnapping of 5 times Italian PM Aldo Moro. Moro, who is about to form a coalition between the right-wing Christian Democrats and the Communist Party, is held for nearly two months before being executed and dumped in the backseat of a Renault, halfway between the Rome offices of the Christian Democrats and those of the Communists.

Thereafter the Red Brigades go downhill fast. First splitting into two ('Militarist' and 'Movementist') factions; then crippled and discredited by police/state/Vatican/you name it infiltration, it fizzles out by 1983; to re-emerge, in part, as the 'Fighting Communist Union' in the late 80s. The man accredited with cracking the Red Brigades, General dalla Chiesa is sent to Sicily to do a similar job on the Mafia and rather predictably gets assassinated along with his wife in 1982.

1979: Europe really starts rockin' again with the emergence of the French urban guerrilla group, 'Action Directe'.

ACTION DIRECTE

Founded by Jean-Marc Rouillan, a veteran of the anti-Franco 'International Armed Revolutionary Group' of the early 70s, and Nathalie Menigon, a former bank-clerk, they set about building up an underground network, financed by bank robberies. At first without much success...

SEPTEMBER: Action Directe debut with the machine-gunning of the French Ministry of Labour.

LATE 1980: After a series of such attacks most of Action Directe find themselves locked up. Rouillan and Menigon are busted when a Lebanese informer lures them to a meeting with Carlos that turns out to be a police trap.

1981: Then President Mitterand comes along, declaring a general amnesty for political prisoners on his election. This is meant to appease Corsican Separatism but it also applies to mainland activists. Rouillan and Menigon and 25 other AD members are released. With this new lease of life, AD get serious, dumping their original anarchist leanings and making links with RAF, BR and Lebanese exiles.

NOVEMBER 1981: A policeman is shot dead during an AD bank raid.

AUGUST 18, 1982: After being declared a banned organisation, AD bomb the offices of the right-wing 'Minute' magazine.

1982/83: AD carry out over 40 bank raids and recruit new members from Paris squatting scene. During one bank raid police shoot dead Ciro Rizatto, an Italian exile from the BR offshoot COLP ('Communists for Liberation of the Proletariat'). In another shootout two policemen are killed.

EARLY 1984: AD bomb ten targets of military significance and assassinate General Guy Delfosse. Then Rouillan and Menigon move their base to Belgium, where they help set up the 'Combatant Communist Cells' (CCC). This is the beginning of a unilateral urban guerrilla movement in Europe, or 'Euroterrorism' as it becomes known.

Gone is the late 60s/early 70s habit of imitating South American guerrilla groups, and also the pacifism of the early 80s anti-nuclear movement. 'Euroterrorism' is a declaration of war against 'McDonalds Imperialism': that is, NATO and the 'Military Industrial Complex'.

JUNE 24: A quarry near Brussels is raided and 1,800 pounds of high explosive and detonators made off with.

OCTOBER: CCC launch a series of attacks on military installations and multinational companies. Their targets include the Brussels offices of Litton Business Systems (designers of the Cruise missile guidance system) and Honeywell (B-52 and Peacekeeper ICM), NATO oil pipelines, US banks and power pylons.

Simultaneously 30 RAF prisoners launch a new hunger strike for political status. After a few weeks the strike is called off, but it heralds the arrival on the scene of the 'Third Generation' RAF.

JANUARY 15, 1985: The revitalised RAF formally announce a pact with Action Directe.

JANUARY 25: AD assassinate General Rene Audran, the head of France's international arms sales organisation, and claim responsibility for the 'Elisabeth von Dyck Commando'.

FEBRUARY 1: RAF assassinate Ernst Zimmermann, the President of the West German Aerospace and Armaments Association, and claim responsibility for the 'Patrick O'Hara Commando'. This really puts the shits up the security forces. Nobody had ever got on with the IRA before.

Zimmermann's wife identifies Werner-Bernhard Lotze and Barbara Meyer as her husband's killers.

APRIL: An AD car bomb goes off outside the International Monetary Fund in Paris.

JUNE: AD fail in an attempt to assassinate Defence Ministry General Blandin, and admit failure in the name of Antonio Lo Muscio, a Red Brigades member shot by the Carabinieri in 1977.

AUGUST 8: A joint RAF/AD commando bomb the Rhein-Main USAF base, killing two people, and claim responsibility for the 'George Jackson Commando' (after the Black Panther leader). To authenticate the communique an ID card belonging to a US serviceman, killed in order to access the base, is sent to Reuters. Throughout 1985/86 there are attacks on NATO installations in Greece, Portugal, Spain, Denmark and Holland, in support of RAF hunger strikers.

Pierre Carette, founder member of the CCC: the group shook their country (albeit Belgium) to the foundations, only to have their logo ripped off by Sigue Sigue Sputnik

DECEMBER: After 25 attacks, the CCC leadership, Pierre Carette, Pascale Vandageerde, Didier Chevolet and Bertrand Sassoye are arrested and events in Belgium taper off to nothing. Guess they must have hit the right four people... In 1988 the four get life with hard labour.

FEBRUARY 1986: 800 supporters of far-left revolutionary groups from Germany, France, Belgium, Ireland and Spain, meet in Frankfurt. But cracks are already starting to show in the RAF/AD alliance. The RAF begin to fall back into old ways, forming links with Palestinian groups, and AD form a 'National Section' in Lyons under Andre Ollivier.

MARCH 1: After the assassination of Swedish PM Olof Palme, an anonymous caller to a London news agency claims responsibility for the 'Holger Meins Commando' and adds, "You can check the history books for why this was carried out." (Palme was PM at the time of the Stockholm Embassy Siege by the 'Holger Meins Commando'.)

JULY 9: For the assassination of Siemens nuclear scientist, Karl-Heinz Beckurts, RAF members pose as gardeners to monitor his route to work in Munich; then detonate a bomb in a peat-turf bag as Beckurts' BMW passes by, killing him and his chauffeur instantly. West German industry offers a £1 million reward for information leading to the arrest of the Zimmermann/Beckurts assassins and the BKA name Horst and Barbara Meyer as the likely suspects.

JULY 21: AD explode a massive car bomb outside the Paris HQ of the 'Organisation for Economic Co-operation and Development' (OECD).

OCTOBER 10: RAF make the headlines again when Foreign Ministry official, Gerold von Braunmuhl is shot dead outside his home in Bonn. Responsibility is claimed by the 'Ingrid Schubert Commando' and suspects named as the Meyers again.

NOVEMBER 17: AD assassinate Renault boss, Georges Besse. (I'm not making this up, honest.) He's gunned down as he's about to enter his Paris apartment block, by two women who make their escape on a motorbike. A French police source says AD are difficult to track down "because they trust nobody, live a life of their own and take just as long as it needs to plan their attacks."

However, by this time the Action Directe star is no longer in the ascendant. Andre Ollivier's 'National Section' is severely depleted by arrests and, after the Besse assassination, the police net starts closing in on Rouillan and Menigon (who is in the frame for the Besse killing).

FEBRUARY 21, 1987: The French anti-terrorist squad 'RAID' storm a farmhouse near Orleans and net the leaders of the AD 'International Section': Rouillan, Menigon, Georges Cipriani and Joelle Aubron (who is believed to be the other Besse assassin). The 'RAID' raid is very popular with the press because Nathalie Menigon 'gave herself away by making regular trips to buy food for her pet hamster' (hence the 'TRAPPED BY A HAMSTER' headline).

And apparently it came just before a major new AD offensive. The police find a list of potential hostages to be held for the release of Joelle Aubron's husband, Regis Schleicher, who is already being held on a double cop-killing charge. Loose-wheel explosives expert, Max Frerot remains at large for some time and carries out a few more attacks, but that's Action Directe's lot. In 1989 the leaders of both the 'National' and 'International' section get life (16-20 years).

MARCH 14: BR successors, the 'Fighting Communist Union' assassinate General Licio Giorgieri, the Director General of the Space and Air Armaments Division of the Italian Defence Ministry.

MARCH 23: A bomb explodes outside the Officers' mess of the British Rhein-Dahlen base during a NATO social function, injuring 31 people. The 'National Democratic Front for the Liberation of West Germany', a RAF off-shoot claim responsibility. But 'War Without End' credits the attack to the IRA.

JUNE 13: Nietzsche-quoting AD leader, Regis Schleicher gets life for the 1983 double cop-killing.

JULY 7: The Canadian NATO base at Lahr in West Germany is badly damaged by a remote-controlled bomb (credited to RAF in 'War Without End').

NOVEMBER 2: During a demonstration at the perimeter of Frankfurt airport, two policemen are shot dead by a Swiss Sig-Sauer automatic (previously stolen from the police). Shortly after, Andreas Eichler, a member of the 'Autonomous Groups', is arrested with the pistol. The 'Autonomen' are a new wildcard development on the West German far-left, specialising in sabotaging nuclear-powered pylons and Green demos, at which they appear dressed in black with balaclavas over their faces, and usually start the fighting.

MAY 1988: Astrid Proll returns to England after an 8 year legal battle with the Home Office and a bit of a press furore. Proll, now a picture-editor on the Hamburg magazine 'Tempo', fronts the 68/88 debate for a dialogue with terrorists, and during a visit to Portobello Road refuses to buy a copy of 'Vague' 20.

JUNE 17: After renouncing terrorism and serving 16 years Klaus Jünschke gets a pardon.

AUGUST 8: The day after the IRA bomb an army barracks in London, there's another press furore over the reported sighting of RAF member Werner Lotze, wandering about Rhein-Dahlen. George Best lookalike, Lotze is wanted along with the Meyers for the Ernst Zimmerman assassination. There's also much speculation about a RAF/IRA link-up to spearhead a 'Western European Anti-Imperialist Front'.

SEPTEMBER 7: Italian police claim they have wiped out the 'Fighting Communist Union' with the arrest of 21 people.

SEPTEMBER 20: Finance Ministry official, Hans Tietmeyer narrowly avoids being shot by a RAF gunman in Bonn.

LATE SEPTEMBER: 5 days of violent protest against the IMF/World Bank meeting in West Berlin, which the Tietmeyer assassination attempt was meant to disrupt.

JANUARY 14, 1989: Former Belgian PM Paul Vanden Boeyants is apparently kidnapped by a group calling itself the 'Socialist Revolutionary Brigades'. They demand a £450,000 ransom, of which two thirds should go to poor relief groups.

FEBRUARY 14: Vanden Boeyants arrives home in Brussels by taxi, and the police refuse to say whether or not the ransom was paid. There are some suggestions in the press that he staged his own disappearance, to avoid a bribe-taking investigation.

SPRING: The end of the 10th RAF hunger strike.

The remains of Alfred Herrhausen's armour-plated Mercedes-Benz

NOVEMBER 30,: As the Berlin Wall and 'Communism' in general starts to collapse, the RAF remind the world that not everybody's happy with Capitalism either: Alfred Herrhausen, the head of the Deutsche Bank – Europe's most powerful commercial bank – is assassinated by a remote-controlled bomb, which blows his chauffeur-driven Mercedes 30 yards along the road in Bad Homburg, near Frankfurt. (Not far from where Jürgen Ponto was killed.)

Herrhausen, the most important RAF victim since Schleyer, was known as the architect of the BRD's financial Ostpolitik and would have been a key figure in the unification of Germany. A RAF note is found with the detonating device (150 metres away from a bicycle packed with explosives which did the damage) claiming responsibility for the 'Wolfgang Beer Commando'. (Beer also died in a car crash in 1980.)

DECEMBER 2: BKA announce that they're after the usual suspects, Barbara and Horst Meyer regarding the 'planning and supervision', and Christoph Seidler for the actual execution of the assassination.

JUNE 6-16, 1990: A series of arrests in East Germany results in the capture of 9 wanted RAF members: Inge Viett, Susanne Albrecht, Sabine-Elke Callsen, Barbara and Horst Meyer, Christine Dumlein (who is later released), Monika Helbing, Ekkehard Freiherr von Seckendorff (the 'Red Baron') and Werner Lotze. Susanne Albrecht says the Stasi (East German secret police) offered her a new life in East Germany in 1980, and told her they disapproved of the RAF's methods but shared its anti-imperialist goals.

JULY 10-16: More wanted RAF members extradited from East to West Germany, including Sigrid Sternebeck and Silke Maier-Witt. In retaliation there's a RAF carbomb attack on 'anti-terrorist expert' Hans Neusel. (Neusel is a senior advisor to Interior Minister Wolfgang Schauble, who himself survives a non-RAF assassination attempt in October.)

AUGUST: RAF launch an anti-unification/'sell-out of East Germany' offensive and vow to step up the struggle against 'a Greater Germany which aims to become a 4th Reich'.

NOVEMBER 12/13: 173 police are injured and 20 squatters arrested during clashes in East Berlin.

FEBRUARY 1991: The US embassy in Bonn is shot at by a RAF commando during the Gulf War.

MARCH 27: 5 members of the Stasi are arrested and accused of training RAF members at the Stasi base near Frankfurt an der Oder between 1978 and 1984. Specifically they're accused of instruction in the use of RPG 7 grenade launchers for the attempted assassination of General Kroesen and the attack on the Ramstein USAF base in 1981.

Terrorists murder man behind Bonn sell-off scheme

By Robin Gedye in Bonn

GERMANY'S Red Army Faction, the Left-wing terrorist group, claimed responsibility yesterday for murdering Herr Detlev Rohwedder, the 58-year-old head of a government-backed agency in charge of privatising or liquidating east German companies.

Herr Rohwedder was shot dead by a sniper's bullets just before midnight on Monday. His wife, Hergard, was wounded in the attack.

A pair of binoculars, a stool and a letter signed by the Faction were found in a garden opposite their Düsseldorf home.

The assassination of one of Chancellor Kohl's most important representatives in the reunification process serves as a clear warning of popular dissatisfaction over Bonn's handling of the economic changes in the East.

As head of the Berlin-based Treuhand organisation, charged with deciding which of

Herr Rohwedder: head of privatisation agency

APRIL 1: RAF assassinate Detlev Rohwedder, the head of the 'Treuhand', the government agency overseeing the privatisation of East Germany. Rohwedder dies instantly when a gunman fires three shots through the study window of his Düsseldorf home. A RAF communique found in a nearby garden calls for a stepping up of the struggle against western imperialism and the concept of a Greater Germany. 'Anyone who doesn't fight dies by instalments.'

Rumours that the Stasi had a hand in the killing don't come to anything, and the BKA admit they have no idea who is responsible. In fact, since the Second Generation RAF arrests in the early 80s, they've failed to convict a single person in connection with RAF attacks from 1981 onwards.

APRIL 25: The BKA finally get a result: the trial of Susanne Albrecht begins in Stammheim. She's accused of complicity in the murder of Jürgen Ponto and in the attempt to blow up Al Haig. Albrecht stands as a state witness, in the hope that her sentence will be reduced but admits to some involvement with the Ponto killing. During the trial it comes out

that Erich Honecker took a personal interest in RAF/Stasi activities; as does the fact that Albrecht returned to East Germany after 2 years in Russia, knowing she would be arrested. But despite playing the poor little rich girl manipulated by the Mansonesque RAF Albrecht still gets 12 years, the same as Werner Lotze.

MAY 16: Karl Otto Pohl, President of the Bundesbank, resigns out of fear of a RAF attack.

AUGUST 7: As President Cossiga prepares to pardon BR founder Renato Curcio, Italian police arrest Carla Biano in Florence under suspicion of planning a RAF linked attack on an American target.

JANUARY 22, 1992: The Federal Prosecutors' Office in Karlsruhe announces a reward of DM75,000 (£20,000) for

Susanne Albrecht

information leading to the arrest of Andrea Klump and Christoph Seidler, in connection with the Herrhausen assassination.

APRIL 13: As a bizarre epitaph perhaps, a letter arrives at the Bonn office of the French Press Agency bearing the RAF moniker and announcing that the RAF are prepared to renounce violence in return for the release of its seriously ill and already long-term prisoners. The letter goes on to say that with the fall of Communism in the East, the RAF has lost its raison d'etre and its support. Klaus Kinkel, the liberal Justice Minister calls for a positive response to the letter and some form of reconciliation...

n connection with a
appings and killings
iticians and bankers

any's Interior Minis-
hael Diestel, told a
ce yesterday that all
living in East Ger-
0 after having been
nities by the coun-
cret police, the Sta-
merged that three
ny Faction suspects
ined at Leipzig rail-
llowing tip-offs to
engers who recog-
from pictures on
. Police said that
ree – Sabine-Elke
Ludwig Meyer and
– offered any re-

now conclusive evidence of a
vilish co-operation" between
Stasi and West German ter-
organisations, but added
there was no evidence yet o
mer RAF members h
worked for the Stasi in retu-
being allowed to seek refu
East Germany.

West German police s
however, suspect that son
rorist actions in the 1980s
have been masterminded
rorists living safely across t
der. In an interview wit
magazine, West German
rior Minister, Wolfgang S
warned that there was a d
the RAF seeking to dev
ther links with some of E

among the radical left

"we miss him."
Unnamed witnesses
claimed Grams was inde

Balaclava gangs ste
up German violenc

MARK FRANKLAND ■ Bonn

TWO shots from a stolen police pistol have
revived the apprehensiv
debate about political vi   German
During a demonstrati
Frankfurt airport last

in itself. ' If nothing gets thrown ', one
debaters is reported to have said, ' faces fa
people go home dissatisfied.'
Although television shows snippets of
violence, both public and politicians seem to
shed it into little-visited corners of the m
's killings have changed that. Thous
demonstrated themselves last w
r cities. Some marched with
ned to their backs. Even conserva
s who tried to soothe them were m
outs of : ' Do something about it, then
e killings are particularly embarrassing f
us Groups support are usually for sterling lef
ng causes   h as 'peace' and th
environ

he yuppie-hating
Germans are back
with a vengeance

**From Adrian Bridge
in Berlin**

EIR favourite weapons are
ks, petrol bombs and beer
les; their favoured head-wear
k balaclavas or checkered
stinian scarves. And, in con-
t to their sworn enemies on
neo-Nazi right, instead of for-
ners, their favourite targets
yuppies, banks, property
culators and anybody who
es to drive a Mercedes-Benz.
or most God-fearing Ger-
ns, the *Autonomen* – "autono-
ts" but in fact a loose collec-
of anarchist-leaning extrem-
– have long been a h
disorder, disru
the horrific e
German nightm
After the initial c
fall of the Berlin
arent triumph of
r communism in
tonomen seem to b
ir feet – and cro
ain. According to the
ice for the Protecti
nstitution (BfV), milit
chists and left-wing extr
mitted 508 acts of viole
first six months of this
ll up on the 354 recorded in
ne period of 1992.
Ironically, the surge can lar
be attributed to the wave
o-Nazi attacks against foreig
that reached fever pitch las
tumn after hordes of right-
···· besieged a hostel

ety," said Tom, a stalwart of the
Autonomen, which is said to number 6,000. "Everybody has to let
off steam somehow. And surely it
is much better to throw stones
through bank windows than at
school mates ... or foreigners?"
It is not difficult to pinpoi
what the *Autonomen* a
they are an

'Terrorist' letter dismissed

Bonn (Reuter) – Germany's
Justice Minister yesterday dis-
missed a letter purporting to
come from leftist Red Army
tion guerrillas that contra
d an earlier RAF offer
ce violence.
etter does not
the RAF b
he from
rou

st-known leaders of the
eading demos against the
ugh they now condemn
a formidable young
e Greens in this year's
ng the party leaders,
State needs ' terror
om its own daily

ch thinking can
various walls :
's police with al
when several
e
athisers met ee
estions that all
ght also be he
oval. hat
ers last t to
ed that ion.
sde a his
cally
to stuck
eness of was
ng the Rhine s and
ain, they would have alike,
that masks are scarcely
who believe they are combat-
n have
GSG-9

More German terror suspects s

From Adrian Bridge in East Berlin

police yesterday
they had arrested
West German ter-
bringing to nine
en into custody
t ten days.

seven arrests in
ours began on
hen four people
een active mem-
e left-wing West
y Faction were
st German city
he-Oder and
hristine Düm-
leased as the
t had expired.
Monika Ha
reiherr von
ner Lotze –

years been high on the list of West
Germany's 30 most wanted terrorist suspects in connection with several muggings, bomb attacks and
murders.
Yesterday's arrest followed
those of two other West German
terrorist suspects living here –
Inge Viett and Susanne Albrecht,
who is wanted for possible involvement in the killing of the
Frankfurt banker, Jürgen Ponto
in 1979. Mr Diestel said initial
questioning of Ms Albrecht had
revealed she was offered a "new
life" in East Germany in 1980 by
members of the Stasi who told her
that, although they disapproved of
the RAF's methods,

From left: Christine Dümleia, Monika H.

Germar
consid
Red A
'surre

Successful' raid may force further

under...
"If the group resu...
it would mark
...period of
...il

cover...
events.
The case has claimed two
heads: that of Rudolf Seiters,
...as interior minister, and
...n Stahl, who was

Shooting mystery tarnis
German anti-terrorist so

CRITICISM of the German élite anti-
terrorist unit continued unabated yesterday after the resignation on Sunday of the Interior Minister, Rudolf
Seiters, and the publication of an official statement which answered none
of the key questions raised.

Mr Seiters' resignation followed
the shoot-out 10 days ago in which a
wanted terrorist and a member of the
GSG-9 anti-terrorist group died.

There have been persistent reports
that Wolfgang Grams, wanted as a
member of the Red Army Faction,
was executed at close range when already wounded on the ground, and
that Michael Newrzella, the member
of GSG-9 who died of his wounds,
may have been shot by his
leagues. Yesterd...
ment, whi...

STEVE CRAWSHAW
in Bonn

The operation was originally described as a success because of the arrest of Birgit Hogefeld, Grams's
girlfriend, who was high on the official wanted list. But the questions
raised about a possible shoot-to-kill
policy have soured the success.

Mr Seiters' resignation may not be
the last. There were renewed demands yesterday that Alex...
Stahl, the federal p...
be forced t...
spo...

GERMANS this Easter are still
struggling to make sense of a
bizarre letter bearing the badge c
the Red Army Faction.
st machine-gun mounted on a fr
'c sided star. The letter arrived
'e week at the Bonn office of Ag
ha France-Presse, the news age
y si A year ago Germany's or
n n tion of the holiday peri
for shattered by news of the k
Late Detlev Karsten Rohwed
re R tbes head of the Treuha
I bee in charge of privatisin
y sta state-owned east Gere
lice fr Shot at his home f
nd Mr Rohwedde

on 27 June at
of Bad Kleine
many, all side
blame one an
Federal Bureau
tion, answerable
istry and run b
crat,' argued
Prosecutor's offic
Justice Ministry
Democrat h
sta...

ed mist shrouds death of an anarchist

An ambush hailed by Germany as a coup against terrorism has turned into a scandal, reports Steve Crawshaw in Bonn

killed by 'friendly fire' (Lah
colleagues, he was not wearing
the bulletproof vest that most
have saved his life...a hear at
least that, as it was a warm day.
...d have been too che

to have committed suicide, not to
have shot himself seconds after
what trying to escape.

A niggling doubt initially occupied that Grams had simply
bled at the 'abortion'. That
seemed understandable, and
...was little question of that
...still appeared to be

the state-heroes. That death-at-a-
...hail-of-bullets version it was,
however, the raw version nobody
seems to believe, officially or unofficially

Witnesses said Grams, himself
wounded and out of action, was
executed at close range. A woman
who worked at the station's newspaper kiosk told German television that she had seen one of the
GSG-9 men shoot him 'a two
...metres from his head' (he
...quoted a w

Germans fear new
terror offensive

GERMAN security chiefs yesterday warned of a renewed wave
of assassination attempts by the
terrorist Red Army Faction in
response to the controversial
killing of a suspected member
last month.

The warning, by the Office for
the Protection of the Constitu-
tion (BfV), came after the release
of a letter from the group in
which the killing of Wolfgang
Grams in the east German town
of Bad Kleinen on 27 June was
described as an execution.

A BfV statement said: "The
RAF is obviously appealing f...
support amo...

ADRIAN BRIDGE
in Berlin

ceded that, with the collaps
Communism, it no longer
joyed any popular support a
its self-declared war against ca
italism had become more or le
meaningless.

Yesterday's letter said: "Th
cold-blooded murder of Wolf
gang Grams has shaken u
deeply. He devoted his life to th
struggle for liberation fr
pression fr...

SELECTED BIBLIOGRAPHY

THE BAADER-MEINHOF GROUP: The Inside Story of a Phenomenon
Stefan Aust (Bodley Head), 1985 (English translation, 1987).

Refreshingly objective look at the subject by Ulrike Meinhof's 'Konkret' colleague and the only person from the Left not portrayed in 'Hitler's Children' as a bloodthirsty nazi moron. Great read, well recommended and unashamedly borrowed from here. Stefan Aust is also responsible for 'Stammheim', the film of the play of the trial transcript; winner of the Golden Bear award at the 1986 Berlin Film Festival.

HITLER'S CHILDREN
Jillian Becker (Michael Joseph), 1977.

The state-approved (and financed?) version of events. The most unbalanced, reactionary, moralistic, right-wing propaganda I've ever read. But it's got some good pictures.

HOW IT ALL BEGAN/TERROR OR LOVE
Bommi Baumann (Pulp Press/John Calder), 1977/79.

"This book should be read by teachers, parents, politicians, and psychologists, police officers and priests to expand their insight and provide information. I recommend it also for young people who, perhaps out of boredom, are toying with the Underground and anarchist ideas." (Heinrich Böll)

CARLOS: PORTRAIT OF A TERRORIST
Colin Smith (Sphere), 1976.

Only marginally better than 'Hitler's Children', but Carlos still comes out of it as a pretty cool guy.

THE CARLOS COMPLEX/ WAR WITHOUT END
Christopher Dobson and Ronald Payne (Coronet), 1977/ (Sphere), 1986.

Ditto. Inaccurate 'Telegraph' view of international affairs but useful for 'Euroterror' events after 1977.

RED ARMY FACTION
(Patrick Arguello Press), 1979.

Communiques and chronology.

THE GERMAN GUERRILLA: Terror, Reaction and Resistance
(Cienfuegos Press and Soil of Liberty), 1978/81.

Interview with Hans-Joachim Klein, whilst on the run from just about everybody, and June 2 Movement and RAF philosophy.

THE HEART ATTACKED
Alison Jamieson (Marion Boyars), 1989
ARMED STRUGGLE IN ITALY
(Bratach Dubh), 1979
ON TERRORISM AND THE STATE
Gianfranco Sanguinetti (Chronos), 1982.

The Italian job; BR communiques and chronology; and Situationist party-line 'on terrorism'.

ANARCHY #38
(Freedom), 1987.

'Armed Struggle in Western Europe': late 80s RAF/AD/RZ communiques/Dellwo/Taufer/Folkerts/Vogel hunger strike in Celle/the killing of Johannes Thimme/'Euroterrorism' and RZ attacks in Düsseldorf and Cologne.

Further articles in: 'THE INDEPENDENT', 'GUARDIAN', 'TODAY', 'TELEGRAPH', 'TIMES', 'EVENING STANDARD', 'N.M.E.', 'BLITZ', 'CITY LIMITS', 'TIME OUT', 'INTERNATIONAL TIMES', 'TIME', 'PARIS-MATCH', 'STERN', 'DIE WELT', 'RADIKAL' and 'TOT ODER LEBENDIG'.

700 000 DM Belohnung